Village Democracy

John Papworth

SOCIETAS
essays in political
& cultural criticism

imprint-academic.com

Published in the UK by Societas
Imprint Academic, PO Box 200, Exeter EX5 5YX, UK

Published in the USA by Societas
Imprint Academic, Philosophy Documentation Center
PO Box 7147, Charlottesville, VA 22906-7147, USA

ISBN-10: 184540 064 X
ISBN-13: 9781845400644

A CIP catalogue record for this book is available from the
British Library and US Library of Congress

Contents

Dedication

**To all who seek to establish democratic,
decision-making power in their
neighbourhood communities.**

Acknowledgements

To the late Leopold Kohr
For the remarkable insights of the most original and penetrating
political treatise of the twentieth century:
THE BREAKDOWN OF NATIONS

To Edward Goldsmith, Jerry Mander, Kirkpatrick Sale
and the late John Seymour for the inspiration
of their published works.

To Peter Etherden, Sir Richard Body, for encouragement
and support, and likewise John Coleman for also
suggesting the title.

To Helen Carroll for careful proof-reading
and to Stella Grimes and Sam Hains for
indispensable secretarial assistance.

Foreword

This book may possibly strike many who first see its title as an extension of the sort of letters one is apt to get which are decorated with copious underlinings in coloured inks. That of course is the trouble with any proposal for comprehensive change in almost any field. Even Beethoven's works were first greeted with outrage in some quarters, and the record is replete with such instances in many spheres. Nevertheless the concept of Village Democracy is an attempt to meet what is increasingly seen as the crucial crisis factor of our times. How do we resolve the problem of the democratic control of power now monstrously centralised, overwhelmingly top-heavy and out of control, and by its sheer scale and technological force, making nonsense of the democratic ethic, breeding unprecedented dangers and putting the skids under any possibility of progress?

It was Einstein who declared you cannot solve a problem with the mindframe that has created it, which is exactly what we persist in doing and why he chose to remark as much.

Our political system is *there;* for most of us it has always been there and we are disposed unreflectingly to suppose it always will be. We would no more question the main lineaments of its existence, however much we may question its workings, than the air we breathe; we accept it as a fish accepts water.

In doing so we are stifling several imposing considerations which we ought to be dragging out into the light of day and scrutinising with all the persistent objectivity that a scientist would employ in tracking down a disease organism. And this persistent refusal or inability to question some of the fundamental assumptions on which our political practice is based is preventing us from seeing just where we are and where we are going.

We are ignoring that its workings have failed to solve a single one of the major problems of modern statecraft; the problem of war, far from being resolved is growing to an ever increasing degree. We may say the same about problems of poverty, health, law and order, education, social justice, monetary and economic instability, transport, environmental abuse, resource rundown, or overpopulation, to name but a few.

Currently our answer to all these and other problems tends to focus on which party or person we should vote for, this, despite the fact that in Britain the giant parties have all taken turns at being in power, or sharing it, for well over 100 years with no discernible effect on the problems other than to make them worse. We might also add the no less significant fact that the programmes they project, or at any rate the ones they adopt in practice, tend to have a marked and increasing similarity.

What is the answer here? If one emerges at all it will doubtless emerge in stages and the first will surely be to realise that we really do have a problem and that it does require an answer. And the problem? That our system of government is dysfunctional, that it is creating or enlarging problems when it ought to be resolving them, and in consequence we should be asking ourselves in what ways we can improve it.

This is actually a rather novel approach; instead of asking which party we should be voting into power we are asking under what system of government we ought to live. It is of course an altogether different question, and if the distinction is not clear let us ask ourselves whether we are altogether happy with the system we have.

Would we, if we were able to choose, find it wise to create a form of government where all the power to govern an entire country is at one centre? In asking as much we should understand that this has never formerly been the case.

There have of course been many governments in the past which assumed powers of life and death over the subjects, where slavery prevailed and so on. People were frequently exploited and degraded to an abominable degree. All this, we may say, was before the advent of democracy, before, that is, people were assumed to have the right to be free to choose. And we have to acknowledge that long before this freedom was achieved the very scale on which life was lived, small, local and non-centralised, meant that many aspects of power were beyond the reach of centralised government. As trade and technology developed an entire class of highly skilled artisans, professional and semi-professional people came into being who exercised their own authority which stemmed from the close relationship maintained between man and work. To this we need to add the way in which most trade and commerce remained local in extent and in local hands.

A central government might be the catspaw of a wealthy land-owning class, it might engage in meaningless wars, it might impose onerous forms of taxation or pass draconian laws to repress the militancy of workers' movements and a lot more. But still its writ had limits beyond which it was difficult, if not impossible, for it to reach.

A rising class of prospering, if not prosperous, artisans made possible the building, furnishing and upkeep of numerous well-built houses which might range from immense stately homes to substantial farm and village cottages or villas. Local life was vibrant with local relationships in farms, workshops, pubs and churches, family life was the norm and had its own determinative effects on the process of opinion formation and the upkeep of a particular but none-the-less general code of values. There were imposing distinctions between good and evil which, however illogical and contradictory they might be, and often were, were not subject to the transient power needs of the government of the day.

The contrast with the disposition of power in the modern world of the 21st century could scarcely be greater or more dangerous. If future historians are likely to marvel about anything at all about this development it will surely be the extent to which vast numbers of people have come quite passively to accept the notion that a central, controlling, national government can be the focus of a quite unprecedented range of powers covering almost every aspect of citizen life and assume it to be a working example of democracy in practice.

It is of course nothing of the sort and even if it was able to demonstrate ultimate degrees of effectiveness in resolving the major problem of modern government it would still be what it is, an oligarchy of centralised power under which citizen freedom of choice is stitched up by a combination of an uncontrollable degree of governmental power, itself serviced, abetted and extensively conditioned by the operations of a highly skilled professional class of bureaucrats.

Is there any workable alternative to a continuous seesaw of rival giant party organisations seeking to control this unwieldy amalgam of power when party members themselves are unable to control their party mechanics owing to the sheer scale on which they operate?

It is a question which ought to dominate contemporary thinking and the fact that it doesn't is part of the tragic disintegration of life and purpose which is has come to afflict Western civilisation. It is the main purpose of this work to suggest an alternative which may at least have the merit of deserving some discussion.

Chapter One

The Global Crisis

Crisis factors: (War – Population – Environment – Resources – Social disintegration) – Deterioration in quality of life. – The dominance of the market. – A transient phenomenon. – Effect of deception on citizen lives. – Economic fallacy of land, labour and capital as 'factors of production'. – Man today merely a consumer. – Citizenship roles – shared responsibility and relationships. – Education in government hands rather than citizen hands.

The modern world is in a state of increasingly dangerous turmoil; its affairs are out of hand and out of control and a stage has been reached where the entire edifice of a commercially dominated civilisation, armed with hitherto unprecedented industrial technologies and weapons of war, is approaching a climax of total collapse.

Nothing of course is easier than to make such predictions; they have been part of the stock-in-trade of judgemental utterances down the ages and the off-the-cuff rejections of such doomsday talk has also its own history of constancy. But how justified today are either such predictions or their rejection? Are things today in such terms really so very different? Or so much worse?

The answer would seem to be, yes, they really are. Doomsday views are not, as possibly heretofore, the province of disgruntled egos deploring that the world is assuming characteristics they may find strange and uncongenial. They spring from a focus on several imposing and objectively measurable trends which are shaping the modern world, and which, despite the advantages they are reputed to yield, are creating immense dangers. These trends share several characteristics; in their modern form they are new, their scale is novel, they are essentially transient, they are inherently destructive and most importantly of all, none of them springs from any widely shared, deeply considered view of what the nature and direction of our societies should be. All of them come, for the most part, from powerful sectional interests. Referred to here is a series of crisis factors:

1.   War and armaments

2.   Population excess

3.   Environmental abuse

4.   Resource squandering

5.   Social disintegration

War

War and armaments may well be the most obvious of our dangers, but despite a great deal of 'protest' action by pacifists and peace activists generally, action having no apparent affect whatsoever on the forces promoting the danger, it is possibly the least considered.

We are clearly moving into a phase of generalised global conflict on the basis of increasingly sophisticated and destructive war technologies in the hands of giant super-powers, and this brute fact has come to be passively accepted as a normal aspect of our everyday lives. The Americans were the first to deploy nuclear weapons in the war against Japan in 1945. It is now known that at the time Japan was already making overtures for peace; the decision to bomb the cities of Hiroshima and Nagasaki, which estimates indicate killed 150,000 in an instant and wounded 94,000, often with intense body burns and radiation poisoning, was quite unnecessary. What then impelled the US government to perpetrate such a barbaric atrocity, surely one of the most savage war crimes in all history?

We do not know; perhaps we shall never know; but it was Bernard Shaw who remarked, 'A nation armed and prepared for war can no more help going to war than a chicken can help laying an egg.' Today, a UN report states that the number of nations with nuclear capabilities is approaching thirty; the number will continue to increase for the simple reason that no one seems able to stop it. The resources devoted to war weaponry and contiguous needs in all major countries continue to increase; each year 'Armaments Fairs' are held where the latest and most effective means of killing the largest number of people are on display, and which their promoters seek to persuade governments to purchase. Destructive potential is obviously approaching some sort of climax; there is, after all, a limit to the degree of destruction that can be achieved before the capacity of the destroyer to enlarge it is itself exhausted.

We learn from the Stockholm International Peace Research Institute that: 'World military expenditure in 2004 is estimated to have been $975 billion at constant (2003) prices and exchange rates or $1035 billion in current dollars. This is just 6 per cent lower in real terms than at the 1987–88 peak of cold war world military spending. As a global average, 2004 world military expenditure corresponds to $162 *per capita* and 2.6 per cent of world GDP. However, there is a wide variation between regions and countries in the scale and economic burden of military spending.

The major determinant of the world trend in military expenditure is the change in the USA, which makes up 47 per cent of the world total. US military expenditure has increased rapidly during the period 2002–2004 as a result of massive budgetary allocations for the 'global war on terrorism', primarily for military operations in Afghanistan and Iraq. These have been funded through supplementary appropriations allocated to the Department of Defence for the financial years 2003–2005 and amounted to approximately $238 billion and exceeded the combined military spending of Africa, Latin America, Asia (except Japan but including China) and the Middle East in 2004 ($193 billion in current dollars).'

What looms large today is the imminence of another global war, and for reasons which relate to all wars of the modern era, there is no *need* for these wars. They do not stem from any personal animosity of the combatants. English and German soldiers celebrated Christmas in 1914 by forgetting all about war and by having a game of football in 'no mans' land'. They did not want war, they did not want to fight, they simply wanted to affirm and enjoy their common humanity; but the powerful, economic and political forces which dominated their lives and which were beyond their control, felt impelled to make war regardless of any expression of popular aversion or of any regard for moral precept. The biblical command, 'Thou shalt not kill' was transformed into the military command, 'Thou *shalt* kill, or be shot for refusing to obeying orders.' The common factor of all modern wars has been the prevalence of conscription and the powerlessness of civilians and soldiers alike to prevent them starting, or to stop them when they do.

Wars in the past were the result of personal decisions by ruling potentates and the motive was generally that of ambition, the desire for more power or to avenge some real or fancied wrong. Those who did the fighting were simply obeying orders. It is only in the modern era that ordinary citizens have been deemed as a matter of right to have any voice in determining affairs of state, or deciding issues of peace and war. Yet the development points to a paradox; despite the development of the apparent voice of democracy and the desires of the ordinary people to live in peace, the war danger has in no way abated. Instead it has assumed increasingly destructive forms of such magnitude that massive armament programmes absorbing a quite staggering proportion of the economic resources of the different governments around the world have now become a permanent backdrop to all our lives.

Why this should be is a matter seldom brought into the arena of political discussion. Ordinary people do not want war, they are the ones made to fight and kill, who endure death of mutilation and whose homes and families are so often destroyed. Yet if they are presumed to have control of their destinies why do wars ensue at all?

We will revert to this problem later, it is one ensuing from the notion that democracy on a mass basis is either feasible or realisable; at this stage we must be content to note the extent to which the problem prevails.

Sooner or later the world will be engulfed in another conflict where these armaments will be used and the kernel of the tragedy will be not that people wanted to start a war but that they had no idea how to prevent it. The problem is part of the general crisis of modern life, and stems from the prevalence of so many illusions regarding the efficacy of democracy when attempts are made to make it work on a mass basis.

Population

The population of China is greater today than the global population of half a century ago. Again we are in a situation with no historical precedent, for China is but a random example of a global phenomenon where mankind's numbers themselves have become a virus of global dimensions. These numbers continue to expand at a prodigious rate in almost every part of the world despite the accelerating death rates from the traditional curbs of war, disease and famine; despite too the greater prominence now awarded to male and female homosexuality. If this latter factor is regarded as one of nature's safety barriers to excess numbers it is noteworthy that many religions continue to oppose it on assumed moral grounds.[1] It is an increase of numbers accompanied by economic expectations of ris-

[1] By July 2005, the world will have 6.5 billion inhabitants, 380 million more than in 2000 or a gain of 76 million annually. Despite the declining fertility levels projected over 2005–2050 the world population is expected to reach

ing consumption standards in relation to car ownership, long distance transport of essential items of food, of expectations related to acquiring TV and radio equipment, computers and to mobile and other telephones. To these factors must be added the demand for housing and for household conveniences such as cookers, refrigerators, microwave ovens, wash machines, toiletries and clothing, and the increasing demand for air travel and mass tourism. Taken together this market expansion of consumerist demand has become a witches' cauldron of problems, problems which are already pressing against the limits of resource availability, the limits of environmental protection from degradation, to say nothing of problems of ordinary economic manageability, and which are increasingly threatening the stability of the productive systems which sustain them.

There is no prospect whatsoever that the vast majority of the global population currently living in primitive rural conditions, or herding in vast, teeming, urban slum areas, will ever come to enjoy, (if that indeed is an accurate employment of the verb), the consumption standards which prevail in Europe, North America and elsewhere. The combined number of these materially richer people is only a fraction of the world total and already the extent of their demands is reaching saturation point in terms of resource availability and deleterious environmental and social effects. The blunt fact is that in many respects we have already over-reached ourselves. Yet all governments of rich countries, with an eye perhaps to the next election and subject to pressures from global economic forces, are geared to confronting these developments not with conservation and a wise restraint, but to increasing 'growth' at almost any cost.

The Environment

It happens to be the only one we have. Yet the current practice is to poison it, to destroy unnumbered species on which the ecosystem is kept in balance, and to pump massive quantities of effluents into the air, which undermine, where they do not destroy, the workings of the ozone layer. The focus instead is on those products such as fish, timber, cash crops and so on which, whilst raising consumption

---

9.1 billion according to the medium variant and will still be adding 34 million persons annually by mid-century. Source: Population Division of the Department of Economic and Social Affairs of the United Nations Secretariat (2005). *World Population Prospects: The 2004 Revision. Highlights.* New York: United Nations.

standards of a tiny minority of the global population, are impoverishing and degrading those of countless millions of others, others whose cheap labour and currently available resources of raw materials, priceless agricultural land and, perhaps above all, water, are already showing signs of having reached the limits of their availability. There is a curious supposition, widely prevalent and by no means confined to science fiction, that when we have finally destroyed the natural basis of any existence at all on this planet we shall perhaps be able to move to another. It springs of course from a realm of fantasy, but it appears to be the unspoken assumption of all economic activity, and of all government policies related to it.

Resources

Our industrial and technological civilisation has been made possible by a relatively plentiful supply of energy, principally derived from coal and oil. Oil is cheaper than coal to extract and to transform into the forms needed to propel machines, so that whilst coal had a head start as the basis for industrial production, the rapid increase in the demand for a ready fuel has seen a much greater emphasis on oil. One result has been the closure of many productive coal mines, despite the availability of reserves. But once a coal mine is closed the workings generally become unusable as pit props are allowed to fall in and working roofs collapse, so that to reopen a mine is a considerable economic undertaking. The former British coal industry is today but a skeleton of its former capacity, just as it is in other important producer countries such as Poland, where many mines have been abandoned. In energy terms oil is currently king, but we have to note that both fuels are indeed a finite resource in what is, after all, a finite planet. This means that exponential increases in demand cannot fail to confront stark physical limits of availability. The early days, when oil could be scooped from near-surface sources has already given way to the need to pump it from depths of three miles or more, and some authorities who have sought to make sense of statistical material are now predicting that oil production will peak in less than a decade.

But it will peak for the first time in oil production history against a backdrop of a continuous exponential increase in demand and of infinitely greater mass-consumer markets in Asia and Latin America which are being 'developed' in a bid to emulate the lifestyle of

Europe and North America, whose populations are of course considerably smaller.[2]

The same authorities have investigated the energy resources to be derived from other sources such as solar power, wind farms and water power, but there seems to be substantial agreement that collectively they can do no more that marginally meet either current or future demands as currently entertained. The verdict would appear to be inescapable, that we are heading for a pronounced energy shortage, one that can only be met by a rapid reduction of demand. It is a prospect which is already overshadowing much official policy-making of those powers, notably the USA, whose economies are based on cheap energy availability. But the policy is in no way concerned to reduce energy consumption, rather it is to maintain and increase it in an insane pursuit of economic growth. One inevitable result is conflict to ensure command of available resources; we can, in consequence, expect more military aggression such as that launched by the USA on Iraq in 2003.

Coupled with the problem of oil is also that of water, an even greater basic resource. An industrialised economy needs prodigious supplies of water in the business of machine manufacture, of chemical processing of materials such as plastics and other basic materials; once agriculture is industrialised, it becomes utterly dependent on irrigation, itself dependent on water supplies far in excess of that required by peasant farmers using traditional practices.

It may be noted in passing the extent to which industrialised farming is dependent on inputs of inorganic fertilisers which in turn are products of the oil industry, and the extent to which increased disease-proneness of the crops being grown by such methods creates a need for a wide range of pesticides, herbicides, fungicides and insecticides (do they not all constitute a cocktail for homicide?), which have a marked deleterious effect on river systems and which, in turn, can scarcely fail to poison water supplies and all forms of life dependent on them. In any case water today has become another

---

[2]   Every day in 2003, some 11,00 more cars merged onto Chinese roads — 4 million new private cars during the year. Auto sales increased by 60% in 2002 and by more than 80% in the first half of 2003. If growth continues apace, 150 million cars could jam China's streets by 2015 — 18 million more than were driven on U.S. streets and highways in 1999.

    The United States, with less than 5% of the global population, uses about a quarter of the world's fossil fuel resources — burning up nearly 25% of the coal, 26% of the oil and 27% of the world's natural gas. (Worldwatch Institute).

source of conflict, as may be noticed in rural areas of China and Russia, between India and Pakistan and between Israel and Palestine. As industrial growth continues at its present exponential speed we must expect, in addition to the social distresses, increased water shortages which swollen urban concentrations will inevitably create, and an increase in the outbreak of water wars.

Social Disintegration

The evidence is all around us. Civilisation does not spring from, nor is it dependent on, industrial growth, at whatever speed it may be essayed; it depends on advances in moral perception and moral practice in the pursuit of truth and beauty. These in turn depend on the quality of personal relationships that prevail and it is not for nothing that the core of the teaching of all major religions is the injunction to 'love thy neighbour'. Ultimately human happiness is not dependent on the extent of personal wealth or the quantity of personal possessions that can be accumulated, or the ability to travel at will to remote places, or the number of fine dinners we may consume. All these matters have their place; a comfortable home and an adequate diet are obviously preferable to homelessness and starvation, but what then is their place?

Do we attain these objectives within a framework of moral imperatives which enhance the quality of our personal relationships and our moral existence? Or do we sacrifice these personal factors to a single-minded pursuit of material objectives? For this is what is occurring. Factors such as growth, efficiency, greater productivity, a higher gross national product and similar economic nostrums have now been elevated to a status of what Kipling once called 'The Gods of the market place'; an elevation reflected as much as anywhere in the record of public holidays. At the beginning of the 19th Century there were at least forty saint's days and other festivals of religious significance in the calendar. In England and Wales there are now only six, and the significance of the nomenclature applied to them is its own testimony to the profundity of the change of outlook. They are now called 'bank' holidays. We simply celebrate the days on which the banks are closed.

It would not be difficult to cite here masses of statistics relating to increases in divorce rates and family breakdown, to the extent to which our hospitals and prisons are getting bigger and fuller, the increasing drug addiction, especially among the younger age groups, the way muggings and street violence combined with drunkenness and violence are becoming part of the normal back-drop of many peoples lives — especially at weekends in urban areas; the increase of depression and suicide, again particularly among the young, the commonplace occurrence of obscene language, the pro-liferation of discourtesy and bad manners, the disposition to revile or abuse what was once held sacred, the growth of cynicism and dis-trust of elected leaders — all too often justified as they make pretence, prevarication and falsehood part of the ordinary coinage of relation-ships in public life.

The blunt fact is that the quality of life, despite, and all too often because of, the elevation of consumption standards to unprece-dented and often excessive levels, has sharply deteriorated over the last two generations or so. Quality is sacrificed to quantity, and quantity is proving to be the enemy of quality to a marked degree. The primary question of 'how good?' has been displaced by 'how much?' and the evidence is all around us in the way people dress, eat, talk, relate, play and behave.

Supermarkets

Any such statistics would need to be considered in the context of how the market is impinging on peoples lives. It is the market which has masterminded the growth of supermarkets and shopping malls, in complete disregard that shopping was formerly, and fairly recently, a social activity. The local shop was run by local people and local transactions would help to enrich local life. Today the remain-ing local stores are all too often simply branches of some giant chain enterprise and the profits are creamed off to some remote board-room where directors commonly vote themselves enormous salary and benefit deals with funds which formerly went to enrich the local community.

Well, of course, supermarkets are wonderfully convenient places, with an immense range of wares from which to choose. What more could one want? the bemused shopper may be disposed to ask. But the real price tag is in the multiple bankruptcies of local, family-owned shops. Perhaps no less significant is the bankruptcy of numerous small local farms. Why bother to pay someone in Wiltshire to grow onions in one of the most fertile areas in the entire globe when it is cheaper to fly them in from Australia? The small shopkeeper and the small farmer go to the wall; what is left is a shop-ping experience where strangers shop among other strangers, pay their bills to strangers, buy their petrol to drive their cars from other strangers and then return home to consume those ever-so-convenient ready-prepared foods and watch television.

And of course the supermarket price tag carries another downer. In perhaps an ultimate sense, and even its more mundane aspects, the quality of life each of us lives is determined not so much by material things as by that ineluctable factor, our personal relationships, and supermarkets are declarations of war against those of the local community. When the local stores are bankrupted, when centralised tax policies combine with giant out-of-town chain shops to make local farming so economically hazardous that if they are not driven to sell up, the farmer's offspring register a determination to devote their lives to anything but farming, where then are the local relationships which were once the moral and psychological backbone of community life?

With these developments the people cease to be citizens, they become customers, clients, consumers; the economic aspect is elevated to an enormous preponderance over everything else in their lives. This is not a matter of citizen choice, but of market forces which regard the matter of citizen choice as a factor to be manipulated with all the skills the advertising industry can deploy.

These forces will argue, as they often do, that the consumers do have a choice and that they can choose not to attend their shops. This is only too true, but it is a truth that conceals a lie, a lie ignoring that human frailties and susceptibilities are being played upon on a mass basis with ruthless disregard of the moral, environmental and long term economic consequences of what they promote. And of course they promote their advertising propaganda over every information channel they can intrude upon, to the extent that the social and educational aspects of people's lives are dwarfed by the consumerist message. And this to a degree that, to take a leading example, the channels of communication are saturated with competitive messages urging people to purchase one brand of car rather than another, whilst the moral, social and environmental consequences of owning a car at all are never brought into serious focus.

Empires

So the market, thriving on mergers and takeovers into ever larger entrepreneurial units that are now global in their range, aided by near miraculous technical means of communication and projection, is aided too by a wanton squandering of resources. It is the world's latest empire, one to which even elected leaders must now bow the knee if they are to attain leadership positions, and which is having a field day as it proceeds to dominate, desecrate, devastate and disintegrate our ancient civilised social structures.

But empires have a way of having their day, they come and they go, as this particular one is surely going. What may be of note is whereas past empires tended to have a lifespan measured in millennia, modern ones tend to reign supreme for a century or so. They do not stay the course. For one thing they have risen rapidly, mainly on the basis of a transient superiority of modern gunpower; but in history what rises quickly tends to fall at much the same rate, and the fate of any global market empire, like that of its major protagonist the USA, is only too likely to be settled in a matter of decades.

But on its way down the concern here is with the devastation it is inflicting on localised social structures, and on this the truth, being a force of its own, has its own way of registering. Despite all the professionalized arts of propaganda and manipulative persuasion, people have taken its measure and are reacting accordingly. They *know* they are being got at, manipulated, deceived and bamboozled, they know an image of the social order which tolerates a powerful medium such as television ought to be in the hands of educators, artists, and others able to elevate the whole adventure of life instead of in the hands of market hustlers concerned only to make a quick buck out of their gullibility and essential innocence. They know, however lacking in the ability they may be to articulate their awareness, that they are being lied to and defrauded of reality, and of course they react accordingly. Some will take the market message at its own valuation, buy their cars and queue for airline tickets to Timbuktu. Others, less equipped with resources, will channel their frustration into Saturday night drugs, drunkenness and depravity as, with insensate violence, they make urban centres ungovernable and as they help to fill our overloaded prisons, hospitals and mortuaries.

Government leaders announce measures to stamp out violence and to curb drugs and excessive drinking, but it is all the stuff of never-never land. This bogus black and white reality ignores that the root of this and so many other problems is government itself and the framework of market dominance and of market values it helps to maintain; a framework that is eroding civic trust, civic responsibility and even civic identity. It is a framework which lacks any moral backbone or purpose other than a determination to pursue self enrichment regardless of any cost or damage to the social framework.

Economic Theory

Traditional economic theory has a fundamental axiom that there are three 'factors of production', namely land, labour and capital, and that wealth creation was the result of a carefully calculated balance of them. To this day the same basic projection is fundamental to economic teaching, despite the results of at least a century and a half of its practice. What is overlooked here is that to remove humanity from the centre of the picture is to lower its status in the reckoning, and that to replace the human-factor-as-cardinal with other factors such as profit or efficiency, is to endorse a process which can scarcely fail to elevate non-human factors to a status whereby humanity is sub-ordinate to them. Labour *cannot* be a factor of production, for if a sane moral order is to have any meaning, it can only be the object of it, and if 'labour', human beings, made, the theologians assure us, in the image of God, are accepted as the object of economic activity, then other factors relating to production must in turn be subordinate. It is a principle that runs counter to almost all current procedures. Work, for example, is not seen, to quote Freud, 'as man's chief contact with reality', not seen as a calling in which refined skills are devoted to the service of others, not seen as a principle means of achieving ordinary dignity, distinction and status, nor seen as a means of sharpening aptitudes for decision-making, for creativity, discrimination, proportion, balance, harmony and self-fulfilment. What then is its point beyond exercising the egoism of selfishness? Modern economics of work are not interested in any such considerations. The person, as 'a factor of production' becomes a tool for the self-aggrandisement of others, is reduced to being a 'hand', and a 'hand' is required only to perform tasks which are pre-ordained by others, repetitive, uncreative and spiritually negative. When human identity is reduced to being a factor of production work ceases to be a calling and becomes merely a job, and whereas a calling is a life-long commitment, a 'job' can, and all too often does, vanish overnight.

This is to question some of the fundamental assumptions on which all dominant modern economic activity is based, because those assumptions are helping to create quite fundamental disorders having ripple effects across the entire social order. For on the same reasoning that the person has become a 'hand' and work a 'job', he has ceased to be a citizen of his community; he has today become a consumer in a mass form of social disintegration. The market forces that displace him from being the central focus in work and production have robbed him of his central role as a citizen. His citizenship has been negated in the economic sphere by a perverse emphasis on his appetite to consume, and whilst the citizen has become a consumer in economics, and an anonymous voter in mass political structures, in both spheres he has been robbed of vital elements of citizen identity. In the matter of consumption in either sphere, whether in shopping malls or public social services, he is no longer a participant, only a recipient.

Citizenship roles do not grow on gooseberry bushes, they are a product of shared responsibilities, of active participation in making decisions and of the personal relationships which are the warp and the woof of vibrant communities and it is important to see the extent to which modern forms of economic and political organisation are destroying even the possibility of such roles. Our shopping malls, where strangers congregate to make purchases from other strangers, have largely ousted the local family-owned (and run) store; giant bureaucratic forms of 'welfare' have abolished any real element of local responsibility, or of any play of the creative powers of local people in making decisions. Railway companies now no longer seek to serve 'passengers'. They are now called 'customers'. It is not our citizenship role as a traveller which is acknowledged, simply our economic significance. Where the citizen once carefully observed the forms of local custom in a multitude of matters dependent on local power and decision-making, he is now all too often reduced to the completion of paper forms to satisfy some remote centralised bureaucracy. Indeed so far has this process of transformation gone that it now dominates and controls not only administrative matters relating to health, police, planning, transport, energy and water supplies, TV and radio, but also the crucial area of education. One would have thought that in such an emphatically local matter, and one so intimately related to issues of freedom and democracy, a really free people would have made it a matter of primary concern to keep it absolutely out of the hands of any national government run by professional politicians. It is proposed to deal later with the question to what extent a political process conducted on a mass basis and dominated by rival, centrally controlled mass party machines, can have any relationship to the practical imperatives of democracy; here it is noted the extent to which the general working assumptions of modern mass societies are not so much buttressing freedom and democracy as destroying them. They are doing so in the name of 'growth' and 'efficiency', but it is a form of circular reasoning in which efficiency is always tied to 'growth', and growth always tied to efficiency, with no attempt made to explain the moral purpose of either. The results are observably catastrophic. As meaningful social entities our societies are simply falling apart. Various sicknesses of mind and body are multiplying, crime is an increasing feature of everyday life when before it was exceptional, family breakdown is endemic, single parentage a growing affliction on the young, drug abuse has become an apparently necessary common feature of our general lifestyle, suicide rates, especially among the young, are climbing and so too are numerous forms of anti-social and generally destructive tendencies of vandalism, violence and viciousness, whether in individuals or en masse.

We have moved into a brave new world where social and family relationships are being sabotaged or destroyed, where dominant economic and political forces are ensuring the instant commercial gratification of individual consumerist propensities, themselves artfully exaggerated to an absurd degree. These are achieved at the expense of the traditional bonds of mutuality and community involvement, so that modern citizen, isolated, manipulated, indoctrinated, alienated and morally eviscerated, is on a doomsday path of social breakdown on a scale which is inevitably matching the scale of the forces which have brought him to this pass.

Chapter Two

War, Democracy & Morality

Why global disarray? – Evidence? – Work of Leopold Kohr. – Aware-
ness of size and scale as key factors. – Success of Schumacher's work and
absence of results on policy. – Why war? – Why other negative fac-
tors? – Modern life out of control. – Play of morality on policy depend-
ent on size of unit. – Definition of community. – Importance of
relationship. – Significance of individual depends on scale. – Morality
a relationship factor. – Democracy a moral objective. – Power relation-
ship not governed by morality.

Any society, as a matter of course, will reflect in its character and its
workings the nature of the forces which dominate it, and these forces
today, anarchic, visionless, rapacious, impersonal, moronic and
amoral, are reaping the fruits of several generations of their dominance in a degree of impending social collapse for which history can
show no precedent. It is possible to view human history as a record
of the rise and fall of great empires which have left a defining mark
on the human adventure. Every continent can show its own achieve-
ments in this regard and for many, especially in Africa, Asia and the
Americas, we have yet to achieve adequate written record. In the
Western world we have seen those of Egypt, Greece, Rome, Otto-
man, the Renaissance, France, Belgian, Spanish, Portuguese and
Britain and we note that however catastrophic their downfall, the
limitations of transport and communication tended to restrict the
immediate effects to the area to which their power extended. This is
not to say that the French or Russian revolutions did not have a pronounced effect on the development of human thinking, but what we
can now see is that all these forms of imperial collapse and of revolution were milestones of failure in the historical record of attempts to
grapple with the problem of power.

Imperial collapse may have been due to internal decay, foreign
conquest, intellectual inadequacy or, as in the case of the British

Empire, a simple failure of nerve confronted with militant native forces inspired by the democratic ideal, but to what extent was the problem of power resolved? Against a rapidly changing background of technological innovation, economic development and the growth of the democratic imperative, it has to be said it was not resolved at all. As we write all empires of power are in the grip of this failure and this is no less true of the currently dominant empire of power of the USA. We may be unable to affirm when or how it will happen, all we can say with certainty is that its day is over because, like all that have gone before, it has failed to resolve the problem of power.

All too often an historic collapse, however momentous, was seen by the ordinary citizen as the transfer of power from one authority to another. In the case of the British Empire the departure of the ruling power was on the basis of the tragic transfer of power to mass political party leaders, such as had evolved in Europe and the USA, rather than to the traditional leaders such as tribal chiefs, which were the product of generations of slowly evolving accommodation to prevailing economic and geographic realities. The result was that a white boss became a black boss, the problem remained unresolved.

We may well ask, what was that problem? And the answer would seem to be the age-old quest for human liberation within the framework of a social order which responds to the human need for justice and freedom. But why today this grim picture of global disarray?

The critical reader may feel that the route by which this ominous conclusion is reached is sketchy at best. Assertions of wide-ranging import have been made, generalisations of immense scope essayed and affirmations ventured backed by none of the rigorous scholarship that ordinary debate would seem to require. Where are the examples? The tables of statistics? The authoritative documents and reports that might have been cited or seen?

Assuming that they are not already part of the background of the reader's general awareness of life, the answer is that all this work and a great deal more has already been done. There is already extant an entire literature of backup evidence relating to environmental hooliganism, to the squandering of our precious finite resources and to the causes of the prevailing social squalor; it is a literature which has already had the effect of profoundly transforming the consciousness of a substantial minority about the general basis, nature and direction of our societies.[1] It may be said to have begun as a trickle in 1962 with Rachael Carson's *Silent Spring*, which sought to indicate the ecological catastrophe we were perpetrating. The trickle became a stream with books from numerous authors such as Edward Goldsmith with, more notably perhaps, his comprehensive survey in *The Way* (1991), which sought to give an overall view of the global environmental problems. The same author launched in 1970 his influential monthly journal *The Ecologist*, which provided a scholarly commentary on developments across the entire spectrum of ecological concerns. As early as 1957 Professor Leopold Kohr published his seminal and outstandingly relevant work on political and economic theory, the most profound volume in its field to have appeared in the 20th Century. It was followed in 1973 by the widely acclaimed 'Small is Beautiful' by Fritz Schumacher, whose diverse collection of essays was based largely on Kohr's work, and in 1980 there appeared Kirkpatrick Sale's monumental *The Human Scale*. These are a few of the main works of what has become a torrent of literature on different aspects of the constantly growing threat of the global crisis.

Mention must also be made here of a more recent volume seeking to convey the awesomeness of the crisis in comprehensive terms by the New Zealand author Derek F Wilson. His *Five Holocausts*, which he lists as militarism, human oppression, economic destitution, the population explosion and environmental destruction, is a list obviously indicating some glaring gaps. There is no reference here to the savage, destructive impact such factors are having on our always fragile social structures, and the extent to which those structures are disintegrating under our noses. Nor to the awesome abuses of economic and political power that controlling forces are perpetrating and which are promoting the evils he describes. He is, in short, focusing on what these forces are doing rather than what they are. He is, nevertheless conveying a picture of which any well-informed citizen needs to be fully aware, and no one unaware of its message can be in much position to take remedial action.

It will be noted these publications were concerned with the effects of modern industrial practice on the environment and to a lesser extent, on the availability of finite resources. Both topics had hitherto played little part in mainstream political or economic debate and this still holds true, albeit to a lesser extent, today. It can only be a matter of time before both factors come to dominate the debate and displace the long reign of class warfare-claptrap, of ideologies related to

---

[1]   See appendix for a partial list of this literature.

property ownership, and such concepts as socialism, communism, 'welfare' and 'democracy'.

The Breakdown of Nations

The displacement will also erupt from another source. As already noted, in 1957 Professor Leopold Kohr published his little noticed work, 'The Breakdown of Nations'. He was by no means the first author to discuss the question of *size* as a determinative factor in the economic and political equation. It has indeed been a theme, albeit a minor one, in much socialist and communist literature, where small-scale structures were seen as an essential attribute of community life. Indeed, towards the end of his life Gandhi had come to see the vitality of village life as the key to the regeneration of Indian polity, involving the abandonment of the concept of a centrally directed and controlled mass national party as an instrument of social progress. Kohr's work was within an altogether different frame of reference; it was in fact a methodical description not so much of the desirability of smallness as an explanation of the inevitable dangers of bigness and those dangers he explained included war, poverty, needless bureaucracy and much else besides. It was an intellectual time bomb and for most people, despite the fact it has been twice issued in new editions, it is still ticking away below their horizons. Despite too the numerical success of the subsequent work by his friend E F Schumacher entitled *Small Is Beautiful*.

Small can of course be quite ugly; nevertheless the phrase struck a chord and the book sold by the million. Despite its lack of structure the book attempted to put the factors of size and scale into the centre of the debate. Unfortunately it seems rather to have stuck there, for after more than a quarter of a century the effects on policy at any level of government are difficult to discern and are mostly marked by their absence, so that currently we are in a limbo of some carefully considered desirable objectives dominated by a determined official thrust in a quite contrary direction. No Chancellor of the Exchequer will fail to announce in his annual budget oration the need for a given percentage of economic growth, and it is not difficult to see that given the general conditions on which the economy operates, given the assumptions on which economic entrepreneurship is based, and the expectations and indeed the need for confidence in continuous expansion on which it is based, he is not free to project any other scenario.

This does not make such assumptions right, it merely indicates their dominance. It is part of the tragedy of modern life that assumptions of a contrary nature, for example the need for conservation of finite resources, respect for the environment, or concern for the vitality of social structures, could not begin to be entertained by the highly centralised forces that now dominate modern life.

Why War?

The concern here is focused on the urgent need for action. There is, after all, a limit to the extent to which it is possible to absorb such a doom-laden picture without asking what the ordinary citizen can do to remedy matters before we are overwhelmed by the catastrophe, military, economic, environmental and social, which is part of the scenario which now overshadows all human life?

War alone is an unmitigated social disaster. The death, mutilation, life-long crippling and bereavement it inflicts, in defiance of all canons of morality, are horrific beyond any reckoning. So why do we suffer it at all? Most modern wars are fought by people who do not want to fight, who would infinitely prefer to be at home with wives and children, who often seek to 'desert' the ranks into which they have been enlisted or been conscripted, and no less often are shot for seeking to do so. Already mentioned is the morally resplendent incident in the first Christmas day of World War One, which saw English and German soldiers seeking to celebrate the birthday of the Prince of Peace by climbing out of their trenches to play with each other a game of football.

The significance of this all too human response cannot be stressed enough; men did not want to fight, they wanted to live in peace and to be friends with each other. The high commands on both sides were shocked at the idea of their men 'fraternising with the enemy'. So the war rolled on and war memorials all over the world today are gathering moss as they continue to testify to the sheer wasteful cruelty of a totally needless war and its unnumbered victims.

So why were men fighting at all? Why indeed has war become a permanent feature of modern life, with periods of 'peace' marked by such massive and continuous programmes of re-armament as to make another outbreak inevitable? Despite all our assumptions and pretensions to democratic governance we have to face the fact that ordinary people today are in the grip of forces they do not nor cannot control. The same evident lack of control pertains no less to many aspects of their everyday lives. People do not want poverty and unemployment, they do not want constant economic upheavals that impoverish their livelihoods. Nor do they want a natural world desecrated by degrees of ecological vandalism which poison land and water, strip the sacred earth of its natural forest cover, obliterates numberless vital species and life forms and in doing so imperils the ecological balance, promoting massive climate disruption and destroying their natural birthright of life and that of all future generations.

Society Out of Control

All this and more is the general lot of humankind today. In posing the crucial question, why? we are confronting the most ominous, the most dangerous, the most pervasive and the most neglected aspect of human affairs ever to have erupted. Our societies are out of control. Just that.

We have to see that lack of control involves some degree of excess, of temperature, of speed and perhaps above all, of size. We may be able to do little about the excessive heat of a giant fire except take preventative measures and get out of its way: we may be powerless in a giant windstorm except to seek what shelter we can, but these are generally natural phenomena confronting us with the problem of adapting as best we may.

But human institutions are human creations, and today we continue to ignore at our peril that it is their very size which prevents us from exercising the due measure of control their workings demand if they are to serve genuine human ends, and if they are to respond to the general moral implications of democratic governance and ordinary human decency. The fact that today they don't is the basic cause of the global crisis and why this is the supreme moral and spiritual challenge of our times.

We are in deep trouble not because governments are 'left' or 'right' or because they are capitalist or communist, or whether they are conservative or liberal or socialist or green or any other name or colour, but because they are too big and their size ignores a warning uttered two or more millennia ago when Aristotle declared: 'To the size of the state there is a limit, as there is to plants, animals or implements, for none of these retain their natural facility *when they are too large'* (emphasis added).

It is the failure to observe the implications of the Greek sage's observation which has triggered the modern crisis and until we begin to heed it we are powerless to affect any remedy.

Community Structures and Size

But why should it not be possible to monitor and manage the affairs of giant states or giant economic forces in order to achieve the goals of human betterment, goals of peace, justice and stable and equitable economic conditions that are so ardently desired?

Perhaps it should first be noted that all such objectives are products of moral judgement involving the application of moral principles. These in turn depend on moral relationships of sufficient strength to withstand forces in society whose play may be either amoral or even immoral. Decent relationships are not accidental superfluities, they are at once the embodiment and the backbone of any healthy and vibrant community life; indeed one may well define a community as *'a social entity in which the personal relationships of its members are the strongest force determining its character'*. Such relationships are of course the seedbed of moral practice; it was not for nothing that Gandhi declared 'You cannot have morality without community'. He was stressing that morality did not operate in a vacuum and it was the personal relationships of community life that enabled it to function at all.

The Mass Society

It is here that the factor of size comes into significant play. People in overdeveloped countries which are dominated by technology have largely ceased to live in real communities; they live instead in *mass* societies and, despite the profound implications to their existence that are involved, it is a transformation the significance of which is almost universally ignored. To this day it is the subject of no serious academic consideration. Books on politics and economics professing to deal with the factors of the global crisis pour from the press without once referring to it, reams of journalistic comment seek to engage with our problems with no apparent awareness that to ignore it simply devalues whatever they have to say, and no leading political voices see fit to give it the least consideration. But the transformation from the personal to the mass none-the-less is there and its most imposing aspect is that the relationships people once had with each other and which were often the functional basis of their morality cease, under mass conditions, to be significant and often cease to operate at all. The reason for this stems from the impact of mass society living on the lives of people in local communities.

Any mass society is the result of the emergence of new, and generally highly centralised, forms of power. These new forms forge their own relationships of a vastly different character from those that people in local communities enjoy with each other and with local institutions.

For one thing the new relationships are impersonal, whereas the former ones were emphatically of a personal nature. This itself is a factor which helped to shape and determine the moral quality of community life, and it is a factor which is enormously weakened and diluted by the mere existence of the new forces.

It needs also to be emphasised that the new relationships are not so much moral as power relationships. Morality is after all a function of peoples' relationships with each other, and because today their relationships are focused instead on institutions or organisations they inevitably become power relations. Relations with members of local, human-scale communities (the oldest social aggregation in history) give way to relationships with *things*.

It should be noted here that whilst relationships between members of a community may be of approximate equality, relationships with an organisation on a mass basis can only be decidedly unequal. Why? In part because the relationship is a power relationship and because on a mass basis power is not in the hands of the individual members but in the hands of those controlling the central levers of power.

Individual Power

The fact is that the larger the organisation, be it a government, a political party, a trade union or any mass body, the smaller the significance of the individual member, and the converse is no less true; the smaller the organisation, the larger the significance of the individual.

It is these facts which destroy the democratic validity of mass voting exercises. The central controlling apparatus may well be acting in the name of millions of 'ones'. It is the centre which formulates policy, arranges publicity, determines who speaks and acts on its behalf, organises conference agendas, determines which matters take precedence in public debates and a host of other factors which manifest *its* power rather than the power of the individual, power which might be expressed through his local community relationships. Democracy on a mass basis is an unrealisable dream; *a mass democracy is an oxymoron*.

The force of this conclusion may be seen more clearly by recognising that whilst human beings may be described as moral entities, an organisation is always a power entity. The organisation may be no larger than the local bowls club, but because it embodies power it will need to have arrangements to manage and control its affairs; so it will have a constitution which will detail how it shall be run, what officers it has, how they will be elected, and their period of office and so on. The grandiose error of nearly all modern political theorising stems from the assumption that a growth in the size and scale of an organisation has no effect on the everyday workings of the democratic ethic, no understanding that the mere fact of a growth in scale destroys it.

How? Democracy is a moral objective. Since morality is a key attribute of the human personality and since the members of a local bowls club will ordinarily know one another, one may be able to say their membership is based on some sort of moral understanding and that it confers on them a working moral relationship. This is surely a decisive aspect of their community life, and one where such moral objectives as 'democracy' can be meaningfully pursued and practised.

To enlarge the scale of such relationships to a giant mass is to effect a near total transformation of reality. For example, the workings of a modern mass political party, which may number millions, becomes an entity where the morality factor has largely been supplemented by that of power.

Whatever moral objectives an individual may seek to pursue by joining a large mass organisation, his relationship with it can only be a power relationship. This is fundamental to his reasons for becoming a member at all; he is seeking, after all, to change the way power in society is used, but his individual power is emphatically unequal to that of the central controlling mechanisms. It is in fact power he surrenders by the mere fact of becoming a member. The same power cannot be in two places at the same time, either a member has it, as in his bowls club by the small size of the club, where his membership is a significant factor in controlling such power as it may deploy, or he doesn't, as in a mass political party where he is an insignificant cog in a massive wheel controlled by others at the centre. The mere fact of enlarged size makes size itself an assault on the democratic ethic as a matter of course.

The fact of an organisation being small does not thereby assure us of its superior moral qualities. There are no straight lines in nature and none in human nature. A gang of thieves will tend to be quite modest in size; all that can be said is that the factor of modest size enables the qualities of the members as expressed in their relationships to prevail. In giant structures those qualities tend to become irrelevant as it quests for objectives related to power, often in disregard of moral factors altogether.

Chapter Three

Mass Politics

Abuse of power on mass basis inevitable. – Mass democracy an oxymoron. – Fallacy of Federal Europe. – World revolution of small nations seeking freedom. – Reasons for poverty. – Example of Swiss cantonal system. – Man not controlling the market, market now controls man. – Factor of advertising and creation of destructive mass consumerist values. – What then can we do?

EUrope

It is in this light one can begin to understand more clearly the full import of some of the abuses of power on a mass basis that have characterised the politics of the 20th century, despite the extent to which people had the vote and could be declared to be living in democracies. The people under Stalin's Russia and Hitler's Germany also had the vote and yet Stalin, with his iron control of a centralised state apparatus, could designate anyone who might oppose his policies, and they were mostly his morally inspired and idealistic fellow Communists, as 'enemies of the people' and have them liquidated (i.e. shot or starved to death in arctic labour camps) by the million. Or we may note how Mr Tony Blair, in the guise of something labelled 'New Labour', could use the machinery of an ostensibly socialist mass movement to fashion an entirely new era of capitalist expansion, consolidation and dominance in modern Britain. How also the supposedly 'democratic' machinery of state in several European countries could be used, largely by hidden forces of money and power, to finance and promote the organisation of a federal European state which will extinguish their sovereignty by enlarging the arena that money power can dominate.

The argument for a federal Europe does in fact embody, insofar as it is ever clearly stated, precisely the sort of fallacies discussed here about the effectiveness of democracy in a giant political unit. It also highlights the nature of the problems giant political units create, not because of any particular political colouration they may claim, but simply because they are too big.

It is asserted Europe will achieve peace and economic prosperity for its peoples. Such an assumption simply ignores the record of every other large federal power in existence. It takes no account for example, that the USA has been involved in every major war of the last 100 years; that China, despite its enormous size and, some would assert, because of its size, has felt impelled to invade and sub-jugate Tibet to many years of foreign occupation, whilst it is now planning an invasion of Taiwan; that Russia engages in a violent war of aggression against the people of Chechnya; or that India has had a military confrontation with every one of its major neighbours since the transfer of colonial power from Westminster to Delhi. Nor is it taken into account that all these giants are armed with nuclear weap-ons of mass destruction, yet still it is argued that a federal Europe will achieve 'peace' even as moves are already afoot to create a Euro-pean military force.

The argument that a united federal Europe will achieve economic stability and prosperity is equally specious and ignores the fact that millions of federal Americans are living below its own defined pov-erty levels, (with over two million in federal jails), that two other giants, China and India are at the bottom of the global wealth league and that Russia continues to stagnate economically in a economic morass of corruption and mismanagement. Perhaps more imposing than the record of the giants as reasons for questioning the creden-tials of the moves for EUrope is the way they ignore that most by far of the wealthiest nations on Earth have populations of less than 10 million. Such unreasonable reasoning ignores that in economic mat-ters, the bigger the ocean the bigger the storms that erupt; that the global economic collapse of 1929 erupted not in Switzerland or Iceland (two of the wealthiest nations), but in the largest open free market in the world, the giant USA.

'Terrorists', 'Insurgents' and 'Rebels'

Statistical material can of course lend itself to a variety of interpreta-tions and it may be observed that aggressive wars and economic mismanagement or poverty are not social ills confined to giant states. Are not many small countries just as prone to militarism or impoverishment as the giants?

This indeed is very much the case and it should impel a closer look at the kind of wars being fought and the nature of the poverty that so often afflicts small countries. More to the point, we should aim for a clearer picture of the forces currently operating in the modern world and not be too ready to accept reports couched in terms of 'terrorists', 'insurgents' or 'rebels'. The fact is that we are living in a transition period where the full force of democracy and the age-old quest for liberty is providing the headsteam for much that fills our newspapers. The failure to comprehend the realities of these events stems from the fact that those who report or comment on them do so through 19th century concepts of statehood rather than the 21st century concepts of democracy.

This failure of comprehension arises in part from the trend of long suppressed national liberation movements to seek to achieve their aims by force of arms. But the language of the gun is neither of freedom nor democracy, rather is it the language of those who control the guns, and those who control the guns tend to be seeking freedom for themselves rather than for their fellow citizens. Every exercise of power leans towards abuse and corruption and none more so than those of gun-play, so that not infrequently corruption rears its head; in different ways, the control of profitable drug trafficking becomes part of the equation and enmeshed in the ambitions and prospects of rival leadership groups, leading to a virtual civil war between factions ostensibly fighting for national liberation. It is a rivalry of which the centralised ruling power is able to take every advantage, not least in projecting the rivals as 'terrorists' or 'rebels'.

Nevertheless we are still emerging from forms of feudal or colonial rule operating on a giant scale, a scale where one 'power' presumed to rule the affairs of many smaller ethnic groupings regardless of their wishes. But the clarion call of freedom is no respecter of feudal or colonial frontiers, which is why the world today is awash with the struggles of subject peoples to attain their liberty.

Many have already done so. Estonia, Latvia and Lithuania were formerly provinces of the Tzarist Empire and of communist imperialism; today they are self-governing, as are the people of Bangladesh, Slovakia, the Czech Republic, Slovenia, Rwanda and Iceland among others. The United Nations numbers today a membership of 193 countries. The onward march of democracy is going to increase that number considerably as the Lozi and the Barotze of Zambia, the Kurds of Iran and Turkey, the Inuits of Canada, the Tamils and the Sikhs of India, the Yoruba, Ibo and Hausa of Nigeria, the Indian tribes of the USA, the Aborigines of Australia, the Basques of Spain and the Bretons of France, to select at random from a wide range of peoples seeking to govern themselves, achieve their dream of freedom.

We are in fact living through a ferment of democratic assertiveness having no parallels in history, one which is repudiating the straight, colonial or imperial lines drawn on so many maps, lines drawn in ignorance or unconcern of the many peoples whose rights to freedom were thereby being expunged. These people, unlike the giants, are not fighting wars to dominate others, they are fighting for the freedom to breathe.

The Principle of Division

And so often the poverty of small nations is the fruit not of mismanagement or misdirection of available riches but grossly unfair trading relations with wealthy and powerful trading nations, of exploitation of their natural resources by foreign companies, often in league with corrupt and oppressive local ruling groups, and often of a sheer lack of natural resources, a lack the quality of mercy exercised by the more fortunately endowed can sometimes do something to alleviate. In this we need to temper our judgement with a grasp of wider considerations. For if small nations are sometimes impoverished and aggressive, let us take on board the full force of the fact is that the *only* nations that are wealthy and peaceful, as well as democratic, stable and tolerant are all, without exception, small.

And one of the smallest is Switzerland. It is also one of the richest, a fact that people tend to assume is why it is well-governed. But, as Professor Kohr was at pains to observe, Switzerland is not well governed because it is rich, it is rich because it is well governed. But what is the secret of Swiss political skills? Why is it well governed? It occupies for the most part a lofty alpine region, one which has compelled it to adopt not the principle of unity, but that of division. Each of its cantons is a largely self-governing unit. This is why the Swiss insist their country is a 'confederation', and the distinction from being a 'federation' is crucial, for whilst the latter is a unification directed from a single centre, as in the USA, a confederation is a largely self-governing partnership of equal members. So that despite the fact that it consists of German, French and Italian speaking cantons, and also encompasses different nationalities and forms of religious belief; despite the fact that such divisions have provoked the most murderous conflicts outside its borders, it has itself been a haven of peace, tolerance, liberty and stability for centuries.

Can we not learn from the Swiss experience? Their system developed naturally from their imposing alpine geography; before modern machine-travel the cantons were often cut off from each other for months at a time and this factor alone prompted the development of a sturdy spirit of independence and self-reliance, so that each canton became accustomed to running its own affairs in its own ways. Alpine height also gave them a certain impregnability to attack and even today, even with modern methods of warfare, it presents a quite formidable target to any would-be aggressor. So that within a virtual fortress bequeathed by nature the Swiss have developed principles of government which may yet save the world from some of the main problems that currently afflict it.

What then are those principles? Whilst elsewhere, almost universally, there has been a constant pursuit of the principles of unity, the Swiss have been concerned to promote and uphold the principle of division. This has enabled them to maintain the general principle of the human scale, a scale of government that does not become so big as to develop a power and momentum of its own which is beyond the power of control of the governed, but which is controlled directly by cantonal and commune meetings in which all are able to participate.

Is it too much to assert that in itself this constitutes the most significant political achievement in human history? To be able to combine modern technology with freedom instead of allowing technology to swamp it, to achieve freedom from war, from economic misery and from the oppression of over-centralised government, is this not what reforming spirits down the ages have quested for? Is it not a road the rest of the world would happily follow, if only it could?

There will be critics who will not be slow to point to what they see as shortcomings of the Swiss system; perhaps it is rather smug, inward-looking and wanting in a spirit of innovation, perhaps it is altogether too content with a comfortable bourgeois level of existence, one which may not be ecologically and economically sustainable. No doubt, no doubt. No system of government can ever be perfect, if only because we are not perfect creatures and every system must have the defects of its virtues as much as the virtues of its defects. What needs emphasis here is that the system works. When, in 1992, the Federal Council voted to apply for membership of the so-called European Community, (by only 4 votes to 3), a referendum in the same year decisively rejected it. The principle of Swiss neutrality, which is a fundamental article of its constitution, was seen as too vital a feature of Swiss life to be abandoned. But the dangers to the Swiss system are only too evident in the development of modern communications.

Democracy and Modern Communication

Today, more than ever before, no man is an island, and the power of indoctrination, especially in the hands of commercial interests and television moguls, to promote values which serve a particular interest regardless of their effect on the general well-being far exceeds that once deployed by the Roman Catholic Church. But whilst the Church, ostensibly at least, was concerned with what might await us in the next world, commercial forces are very much concerned to condition our appetites in ways which will enrich them in this, and regardless of the price they exact. And if that price involves the surrender of national identity to some European super state, or the satiation of consumerist appetites by an ever closer integration into global markets at the cost of national economic independence, that price will be paid if the market has its way.

The lesson to be derived from these considerations is that markets are not natural phenomena to the laws of which we should never hesitate to genuflect, they are man-made artefacts and can be regulated by man-made measures if we so desire. But in this case such regulation can only be achieved effectively if the scale of the market is appropriate to the scale of man himself. Once that scale is abandoned we are at the mercy of 'market forces'. We are no longer controlling the market, the market is controlling us. The factor of scale is not some fringe consideration, it is determinative.

With regard to EUrope it is noticeable that not a single local branch of any political party, trade union, cooperative union or any representative body of citizenry of any European country has called for a federal Europe. It is a call manufactured by the power of money to serve the interests of such power; it is a massive advertising campaign financed by the citizens' own tax monies to persuade millions of innocent, gullible souls that they will be able to live the life of Riley and peace forevermore if only they will put their necks on the block.

The Supremacy of Values

Perhaps these considerations help to give a clearer picture of the reasons why a global crisis exists at all. Why the scale and violence of armaments is increasing annually by leaps and bounds so that another world war is inevitable if we do not change our ways. Why economic and industrial activity is assailing the life-support systems of the planet to a degree that it is likely to overwhelm the entire adventure of civilisation if not soon drastically halted. And why wealth increases for a relatively rich minority whilst the majority of humankind is afflicted with ever increasing degrees of destitution because of the way wealth is generated and traded.

The supreme power of modern societies resides not in money or in those who succeed in climbing to the top of the greasy pole of political authority, it lies in the values by which people have come to live and no remedy is possible if we fail to take full note of the nature of those values and how they are promoted. It is a statement of the obvious that today those values are inherently destructive, for they centre to the exclusion of most other considerations, and not least the exclusion of moral considerations, on the propensity of the individual to consume the products of market operations.

'I consume, therefore I am' has become the inarticulated philosophy of millions who drive around in cars, shop at giant supermarkets, elaborately furnish their homes with mechanical artefacts, fly to remote places for 'holidays' and generally, by the values they adopt, however unwittingly, make their contribution to the mordant peril of the global crisis.

What then is the origin of the dominance of these values? It is not so long ago, almost within living memory, that the values of a local community could be said to have been formulated from three major sources. There were first the teachings of the churches and religious bodies. Then there was the civic authority, the structure of parliament, the monarchy, the military and local political and judicial structures. Lastly there were the personal relationships of people themselves, bearing in mind that local farming, workshops and trade were still largely in local hands and that the role of work in their lives could not fail to have its own influence in formulating and affirming the values by which they lived.

All this has largely been swept aside; local communities as meaningful and powerful forces in determining social and personal priorities have all but vanished in the anodyne market acids of the mass society. Society itself has largely abandoned the idea that its overall governance rests on fundamental beliefs relating to the transcendent mystery of life; attempts to relate to its nature in ways which might give dignity, even perhaps nobility, and certainly a sense of assurance and fulfilment, have been relegated to the current cant formulation that society has become secularised, a statement which begs all the questions whilst failing to answer one.

The idea that authority, whether civic, parliamentary, royal, ecclesiastical, judicial or military, somehow represents the collective consciousness, identity and direction of society, and is accordingly given some due deference, has all but vanished as mass man has emerged, tabulated and regulated as he swans his way along to a destiny he has neither designed nor desired and which, unless he rapidly changes course, will encompass him in a social collapse of quite unimaginably tragic proportions.

Chapter Four

Which Path?

Tragic consequences of mass scale reformism. – Need to take stock and consider new power structures. – What size of political and economic units can people control? – Element of compulsion in leadership roles. – It is not what leaders do, but what they are. – Problems of 'regional' government. – Need for appointments from Downing Street to be replaced by elections from local sources. – How do we achieve local power?

Mass Perils

Clearly the world is in the midst of an utterly unprecedented global crisis; we have sought to indicate that the forces which have helped to unleash it are out of control because their very size and scale make it impossible for them to be controlled for sane social purposes by anyone, not even by those who are ostensibly purporting to be in control. They too are out of control and perpetrating mischief because in the grip of market forces they must, knowing that if in their leadership roles they seek to pursue contrary or alternative courses, they would simply be replaced by others of a more market conformist disposition.

Since the factor above all which has enabled the crisis to assume the size and force of its current terminally dangerous extent is that of size itself, so that the traditional, organically structured, power-dispersed framework of life of former times has been largely supplanted by *mass* forms of society, it is clear that any attempt to remedy matters on a mass scale are foredoomed to failure.

In asserting the key role of mass forms of organisation in creating our current dangers it needs to be emphasised that it is not any particular mass organisation, or of any particular political or economic purpose which is the danger, rather it is the fact of the mass scale of organisation itself.

One reason for this, as we have noted elsewhere, is that the larger any organisation may be, the smaller becomes the significance of each individual member. The converse of this is no less relevant; the smaller the organisation the more pronounced is the significance of the individual member. The voice of one person in a ten-member committee may be taken as being of far greater significance than that of one person in a ten thousand crowd chanting a slogan.

It may be asserted that even in a mass organisation individual judgement, and therefore control, prevails by the exercise of voting procedures. It is an assertion voicing one of the most dangerous and prevalent misconceptions of modern political realities.

The existence of any mass of people betokens the need for some controlling or organising structure concerned with the achievement of its objectives. Whether that structure is itself governed in ostensibly democratic terms or not, that organising and controlling will be done from some central focus, a focus in modern conditions which will embody a variety of pressures, processes and procedures which themselves will embody the power that the structure represents. That focus will also have access to a range of facilities, office equipment, communications, media contacts and financial resources not generally available to the ordinary member. Yet the assumption prevails that that power is controlled by the members regardless of the fact that on a mass basis this is not only extremely difficult but generally, as the Russian communists under Stalin discovered, impossible.

As we write a Labour Party Annual Conference is in progress. The current political agenda is dominated by the decision of the Labour Prime Minister to go to war in Iraq; a decision now increasingly viewed as disastrous, and it is highly probable that if a conference motion were tabled that British troops should be withdrawn that, to the acute embarrassment of the party leadership it would be carried by a massive majority. Despite the fact that a number of local parties have in fact put forward such resolutions, nothing is easier, despite the fact that the question is currently central to British political life, than for the central party bureaucracy to ensure that no such motion will appear on the conference agenda.

Stalin's methods of control were rather more direct; as noted earlier, when confronted with an imminent threat from Leningrad delegates to unseat him at an impending party conference he had them all arrested as 'enemies of the people' and shot.

These bleak instances may serve to indicate the extent of the power being exercised by the centralised controlling functionaries of any mass organisation. They, whether appointed or elected, control the mass party information channels, the conference arrangements, the promotion prospects of persons within the hierarchy, the degree of publicity exposure that given persons receive (or do not receive) through party channels, the budget allocation for specific party activities and so on.

Mass involvement in any matter is apt to be spasmodic, fitful amateur, peripheral, ill-informed, sometimes mistaken and even counterproductive of its real interests and objectives, whereas the forces at the centre will be persistent, professional, fully targeted on where its interests lie and no less fully aware of the intricacies of bureaucratic structures and where and how influence may be deployed to achieve particular objectives.

These forces at the centre will have no other daily concern but to ensure the predominance of the power the central structure embodies; whilst the individual member will have a living to earn, the preoccupations of family and social life and even membership of the other organisations; in this light it is easy to see that far from ensuring a democratically equal sharing of power, membership of any mass body is an active ingredient for the disempowerment of the individual.

But what may be clear in terms of logical reasoning has not been clear to others seeking to change social structures, such as revolutionary or radical social reformers. They have sought persistently to effect changes on the same mass scale that has promoted the problem. They have failed to recognise that in modern times it is the mass scale itself which is the primary problem and that if they are serious about their quest for change all their focus needs to be not so much on what governments *do* but what they *are*.

They are too big, as the late Professor Leopold Kohr was constantly at pains to urge. Even at the price of oversimplification his observation holds: 'Whenever something is wrong something is too big'. Such wisdom has not modified the zeal of the reformers to seek to effect changes on a mass scale, so that modern history is littered with the tragic consequences of their failures. There have been mass movements galore, mass revolutions, mass campaigns, mass protests, mass voting exercises, mass parties, mass peace movements and mass manifestations of popular concern or discontent across the entire spectrum of political and social life and all of them have ended in failure.

The world today is in far greater danger from countless forms of excess being perpetrated on a mass scale than it has ever been; so great indeed is the danger mass government and mass organisation has created that today the very existence of the human race as a species is now imperilled. The Astronomer Royal recently declared the chances of human survival by the end of the present century are only 50:50.

It is time now to call a halt, to take stock of where we are and to recognise the real nature of the forces that have created our present peril; time to identify those forces, time to reject them and time to build new structures that serve genuine human needs before the consequences of the present structures overwhelm us.

Market Values

What is involved here is the challenge of a major transformation of present systems of power and authority, one which recognises the dangers of the present top-heavy, over-centralised, over-large and essentially authoritarian and destructive arrangements, and to seek to replace them with structures which are amenable to our general long-term needs, and which are responsive to the criteria of citizen moral judgement. The global crisis has erupted because none of these considerations is being applied to the everyday working of our political and economic institutions. Our political processes have been suborned to the imperatives of powerful commercial forces seeking immediate gain regardless of any long-term consideration as they affect the general well-being.

They have been enabled to achieve their pre-eminence over citizen political judgement and power by the sheer scale on which they operate to promote their own market orientated values. Their power is of a scale and a strength, operating from highly centralised vantage points, often well hidden from general observation, which makes them masters of the scene.

Very few people appear to have grasped the full nature of this development, how it so forcefully impinges on the highly centralised political processes as they prevail in most developed countries today regardless of any ballot box results, and how, as the real masters of the political scene, the very nature of competitive market forces impels them to ever greater expansion of entrepreneurial initiative regardless of the tragic outcomes of war and of environmental and social disaster. If we are to counter these forces with new ones that will enable the force of citizen judgement to bring them under control, rather than be controlled by them, what form shall the new ones take?

Appropriate Size

It becomes again a question of size; what is the largest unit of political and economic power over which the citizen can exercise enough control to ensure that citizen interests are served rather than abused or ignored?

There is currently a great deal of focus on the idea of regions and regional government, much of it being promoted by the gravy-train riders in Brussels. It must be over forty years ago that I had a discussion with a Catalan nationalist in Spain who was arguing that his movement supported 'Europe' because it would enable the Catalans to get Madrid off their backs. When I suggested that it was simply a question of jumping from the frying pan into the fire, he seemed quite unmoved and was sure they would be able to hold their own against anything coming out of 'Europe'.

One would like to think a greater degree of realism has since come to prevail. It is not simply that the overpowering stench of corruption that now chronically seeps out of Brussels is so manifest, it is an awareness that the objectives of the unelected upstarts in Brussels are not only different, but quite opposed to the concerns for liberty, democracy and independence that have inspired the moves for regional autonomy in both Europe and across the world.

And it is no use blaming or campaigning against particular political leaders or boardroom tycoons; they act as they do because they must; if they act otherwise they are ousted, as Mrs Thatcher discovered after her anti-EUrope speech in Bruges in September 1988. And just as governments must have a continuously expanding economy if they are to fund the social service goodies that create the electoral favour that keeps them in office, so boardroom tycoons are only too well aware that the price of failing to pursue ever greater expansion and ever bigger profits for their particular company is a predatory takeover or merger from rivals, or bankruptcy.

Again and again we must insist that our focus of concern is not knee-jerk reactions to what such people *do*, however monstrous, but what they *are* and what they represent. Since they represent forces far too huge to be susceptible to ordinary citizen control or citizen moral judgement we must expect multiple evils to ensue as a matter of course; our focus needs to be on scaling down the size of both government and market operations to one that makes them manageable in democratic terms.

Organic Political Structures

Does the idea of regional government answer this need? It clearly
depends on several factors. The first is size, and this in turn relates to
geography and demography. If the 'region' is so large that the inhabitants are unable meaningfully to relate to each other and so exercise
normal democratic control over their common affairs, then we are
confronted with the same problem as that of a giant nation.

In the USA there is an excellent organisation which promotes the
concept of 'bioregions', regions which have a unity of natural fea-
tures such as topography, water systems, flora, fauna and so on,
which ought to be self-governing entities. It is an admirable concept,
but attempts to apply it to England lead to the awareness that some
US bioregions are larger than England itself! This does not of course
invalidate the concept, but it points up the importance of having
regard to size as a determinant factor of a 'region'. Size, of course,
also relates to a second factor, that of numbers; is a city a region?
Even if its population is larger than that of some countries? Populations of urban cities today are often counted in millions, which gives
emphasis to the crucial nature of a third factor, which is, who
decides?

Is the region designated as such by some higher authority above?
Or is it the product of the organic grouping of numerous self-regulating communities from below? That is surely the crucial test.

Hence the need to seek structures which are locally based, locally
focused, locally funded, locally empowered and locally operated
and controlled, that ensure that local people make the everyday
decisions within the province of local life, and that they choose
elected representatives who collectively manage all services of
wider or regional remit. It is a transformation which needs to take
full account of the presently grotesquely top-heavy nature of government patronage power. This is now wielded over an entire
swathe of essentially local functions and offices ranging from gas
and water services to broadcasting, TV and telephones. The members of the boards which exercise control over these and many other
matters are today largely appointed from Whitehall, a process which
reminds us that effectively we are governed by an oligarchy of officials. What characterises them is their remoteness and their anonymity, so that the citizen disposed to bestir himself to question their
proceedings will find himself devoting an inordinate measure of
time and trouble in doing so. He will be discovering the penalty
exacted when the cardinal democratic rule, that the line between

government and the governed should be as short as possible, is breached. Since that line appears to be quite the opposite and to be as long as possible, the need for fundamental change is surely self-evident. The power of appointment to boards controlling local matters needs to be quite unequivocally in local hands and subject to local recall.

Hence there needs to be an urgent review of the powers of all authorities so that those powers stem directly from local electorates and are answerable to such electorates in such fields as:

1. Education
2. Radio & TV
3. Police
4. Planning
5. Transport
6. Finance
7. Taxation
8. Water and sewage
9. Health
10. Currency
11. Gas & Electricity
12. Postal Services
13. Judiciary

Such an approach involves a need for national governments to be stripped of all local powers they now possess so that they are confined essentially to matters which are of national concern. This latter qualification rests on the principle that their functions are confined to those matters clearly beyond the competence of local or regional councils and might well include:

1. Defence
2. Foreign Affairs
3. Supreme Court
4. Trade
5. Civil rights
6. Immigration

It will be obvious that what is proposed here is a transformation of powers which match the extent of the perils the continuance of present arrangements are promoting. It is not a blueprint; it is a modest attempt to stake out the kind of changes we need to survive, as much as it is a call for a vigorous and thorough-going debate on the direction we need to take.

That direction will need to incorporate yet another factor, that of economic self-sufficiency. No social unit can claim or expect to achieve to achieve a vibrant democratic form of government if it is dependent for its everyday sustenance on sources over which it is unable to exercise its own control.

The political problem revolves around the problem of power; who has it? Who decides? In whose name and for what purposes is it deployed? If global economic forces are determining something so basic as whether or how, the members of any social unit are fed, it is those forces which are the masters of the political process. Paupers can hardly expect to be practising democrats when their very means of livelihood are controlled by others.

Global market forces depend for their success on producing as cheaply as possible and selling at the highest possible price; these considerations cut right across concepts of regional independence. The cheapest labour markets today are outside, let us say, Europe and the USA. The dependence of any particular region in these areas for, again let us say, rice, textiles or manufactured goods, on sources controlled by globalised commercial concerns, cannot fail to make such regions dependent on them rather than on their decision-making processes.

There is much to be said for trade in surpluses and non-basics, but to be dependent on external forces for the fundamental means of subsistence is to surrender the power to control a region's own destiny. In this context it needs to be seen that the vast swollen urban complexes that today claim to be cities are really transient hostages to fortune, sooner or later and it is always later than we think, the factors that make international trade possible at all, oil and other resources, transport, market confidence and a blind confidence by both producers and clients in market assumptions on such a scale as now prevails are likely to prove as transient and ephemeral as a weather report when the bubble of international trade finally bursts (and is there really anyone sanguine enough to believe it won't?) we must expect trouble on the scale of the forces now operating have created.

So much of human history, and our view of it, has been conditioned by the existence of small populations and abundant resources, factors which have helped to create the illusion that whatever we are or do there is always plenty more out there. In the 21st century our numbers have swollen to unprecedented and formerly unthinkable degrees whilst our demands for material resources, both individually and collectively, have expanded to such an extent as to be quite unsustainable and a precursor to an era of acute shortages of basic needs.

It is one of the ironies of contemporary events that in some relatively well-to-do countries some well intentioned idealists have helped to popularise a slogan abjuring 'Make Poverty History'. They appear to be quite unaware that we are on the threshold of one of the most devastating disasters ever to have afflicted humanity in all its history, a disaster in which millions, and probably billions, are going to be victims of famines, wars and diseases. This is not guesswork but a reference to events already in train, the work of forces far too enormous to be controlled by anyone for anything.

How?

This raises the question 'If localisation is our route, how do we set about traversing it?' It is indeed the question of the hour. How? How, for that matter do we proceed to make any changes at all that are likely to prove effective in checking, far less reversing, our current Gadarene rush to a precipice of unmitigated disaster?

It will help perhaps if we take note of our current practice in seeking change. Anyone seeking to act today can be counted upon to be invited, indeed urged, to join an organisation. Since it will generally be a national, centrally organised, mass organisation, he will at once be confronted with all the dangers, failures and ineffectualities of any mass organisation as indicated above.

Or he will be invited to subscribe to a publication, one with such a huge readership it will carry all the same considerations of one individual as a member of a mass seeking to influence a centrally run body. Or it will be one of such tiny outreach it only reaches a limited body of those already converted to the cause and who essentially are simply talking to each other.

Or he will be invited to join massive street demonstrations of protest concerned to express disapproval of a particular, and generally transient, governmental policy move, perhaps a war, a new tax, a new weapon, genetic engineering or whatever. Often these protests are focused on some abstraction such as 'peace', not something likely to gain much attention from the passive millions of our mass membership societies, or to be of more than passing effect.

Such moves spring from an essentially 19th Century mindframe, as do proposals for letter-writing campaigns to members of parliament, or for mass parliamentary lobbying. They are akin to seeking a cure for a diabetic condition with a sugar-based diet. Another recent move involved urging M.P's to set up a special ministry of 'peace'! One having all the gallant insouciance of a request to the Federation of British Butchers to establish a branch of The Indo-Pakistan Vegetarian Society.

All such moves are the product of countless individuals who are aware of the dangers we now confront, individuals often imbued with an uncommon degree of disinterested idealism and of a readiness freely to devote time, resources and even their lives to the great cause, whilst lacking the most rudimentary appreciation of the real nature of the problems confronting them. They seem to share a common assumption that in political and economic affairs the shortest distance between two points is always a straight line, and they proceed on it in defiance of all the lessons of failure and ineffectuality that now stare them in the face.

They fail to grasp that the problem is not in itself war, or capitalism, or global economic brigandage, or this or that president or prime minister. Is a crisis of power, power of such huge aggregates that it is beyond our control. It is running amok and defying all moral principles that may check its course, defying all the accumulated moral wisdom of former ages, defying rationality, common sense or regard for the well-being of the planet and its inhabitants, both present and of all generations to come. And since it is above all a crisis of power it needs to be at the top of the agenda to determine how power may be restored to human control if events are not to provoke a general nemesis over all our endeavours.

Chapter Five

Making Local Government Local

Bioregions? – Do they enable democracy to Function? – Downgrading of local government. – Inefficiency and expense of national ministries for local services. – National ministries for local problems divert attention from National problem. – No real difference between giant parties. – Threats to freedom. – Need for restoration of local power. – New forms of power all centralised. – Surreal mindframe created by advertising.

Parish Assemblies. – Role playing with a difference. – Dangers of economic collapse. – Lack of statesmanship. – The role of the party machine. – Financing of mass parties. – Power, not moral bond, between government and the governed. – Lack of regard for positive health promotion. – Role of the Church.

Local Power

It will be clear from the foregoing that any practical proposals which do not focus on the problem of power and of ways of securing control of its play can scarcely amount to a solution and are only too likely to serve as little more than a distraction.

If power is to be transferred to the people in such democratic terms that people themselves do make decisions now taken by remote centralised authorities, authorities which are generally beyond the effective power of the people to influence or to prevent abuse, we have to envisage the creation of new forms of authority at the base of our society and ones of which the people can show themselves to be the masters.

If the plea for bioregions as working entities of government is accepted, and few people of any perception can fail to see that the focus it promotes on the natural environmental factors is likely to be infinitely more workable and acceptable than giant, centralised, mass governing bodies, especially when these are dominated by

market forces which are content to ignore environmental considerations altogether, we have to ask whether it does answer the crucial
need for human control?.

When humans take care of their environment there is far more
chance that the environment will sustain them than if they ignore or
abuse it, is a syllogism that need not be questioned. But does the size
of the bioregional unit, in itself, enable the creative energies of individual citizens to be harnessed for sane social purposes in a decisive
way to ensure they prevail? Or is this likely to be yet another example of the Fabian top-down disease of auntie-knows-best, regardless
of peoples' wishes even when relating to all-important questions of
the environment?

What confronts us here is a need for a new approach, one which
has its roots in the history of community life across the world. At
present local government in Britain, as in many other countries, has
been virtually regulated out of existence and replaced by local
administration run from Whitehall; it has become an accepted pattern that the central government not only determines the limits of
local government, but actually runs many local services itself. This is
notably true of education and of what is called 'health' services.
Local community boards or committees which formerly ran these
and other services and helped to organise fund-raising activities to
finance them, giving their services freely, have been wiped out of
existence. In this context we should note the extent to which the
fêtes, carnivals and other events they organised were themselves
important means of strengthening community bonds and concepts
of community service. They have been replaced by huge centralised
bureaucracies which have proved as inefficient as they are expensive, if only because administrators in centrally located offices are
grappling with problems which can only be effectively resolved by
local people who, after all, are best placed to deal with their own
local problems. These local hospital committees, school boards,
boards of guardians to care for orphaned children and other largely
voluntary community authorities have been displaced by a 'national' health service, a 'ministry' of education and 'ministries' for
social and other services. Newspapers unceasingly report how one
aspect or other of these services is breaking down or failing to
achieve the results required; rival political factions have a continuous field day in castigating the faction in power for its failures whilst
promising to do ever so much better if the electorate would only vote
them into power, prompting the faction in power indignantly to

deny anything is seriously wrong and that anyway they are going to vote much larger sums of taxpayers money to improve matters.

Village Power

The fact is that it matters little which faction controls the strings; in seeking to deal with such matters on a centralised basis which makes their problems unresolvable, power factions are achieving two things. They are diverting attention from their far more serious failures in other spheres more properly their concern, their failure to prevent war, for example, or to safeguard the environment, to halt the excesses of global trade which are further impoverishing countries already mired in poverty, and, in the UK at least, they are failing to uphold the political independence of the country they presume to govern in the face of the threats from international capital centred on Brussels, or to protect the country's agriculture and its fishing industry.

No less important, their blind arrogance is serving to destroy the cohesion, the vitality and even the identity of local community structures. Instead of fully relating to each other people are being compelled to relate to the agents of remote government ministries who are usurping the natural authority of local people to govern local affairs themselves and in doing so, assisted by mass motoring, out-of-town shopping malls and centrally controlled TV, impelling them to become strangers to each other rather than neighbours.

Nor should we overlook the threats to freedom that necessarily accompany such a distorted dispensation of power. It is, after all, the main function of government to embody the power to govern, and one of the chief problems of ensuring that it operates democratically is to ensure its power is responsive to the will of the governed. One of the great, unlearned lessons of modern life is that on a *mass* basis this is impossible and no amount of ballot-box mongering can achieve it.

The power that exists in any agglomeration of human life is a dangerous power; it can start wars, it can destroy freedom, it can embark on policies which result in the murder of millions of its own subjects, it can manipulate media power to promote an utterly false image of its own objectives and endlessly tyrannise, deceive, distort and abuse the public interest. These are not mere generalities; they are the stuff of modern governmental history and if we heed its lessons we need to acknowledge that central government power should be confined to those functions that are strictly related to central government matters and that it should not be allowed to be exercised beyond them.

What confronts us is a need to restore local democracy, to restore to elected local village and parish bodies not only the powers that have been filched from them over the last century or more, but to assume responsibility for the new forms of power which have burgeoned over the same period and which are impinging on local life in ways which are currently beyond local control.

National Government Versus Community

What is significant about these new forms of power is the way in which in almost every respect they have increased the power of the central government, whilst weakening the power of local communities. The most obvious of these new forms are transport, communications, planning, radio and television, computers, mass production, mechanised agriculture, credit card and large-scale banking and the development of international trade. In almost every respect, where any form of governmental oversight is involved, it is central government that does the overseeing. And the same is true of such matters as welfare provision.

It may seems a very long time ago that each local community organised and funded its own provision for sickness, homeless children, poverty, the aged, the blind, the halt and the lame, but in Britain it is still within living memory. There were Boards of Guardians and a wide range of local charities that catered for those in need or who were socially distressed or disadvantaged. The work of these agencies may have been piecemeal, uncoordinated, socially hidebound and imperfect; they may well have been quite inadequate in coping with the degree of social distress the new age of machines had engendered, but all too often their work simply reflected the ruling ideas of the time and by and large, until the new forces erupted, they worked.

The previous chapter is headed 'Which Path?' and throughout the preceding chapters it has been urged that the failure to take proper account of the factors of size and scale is one of the main reasons for the emergence of the global crisis, so that centralised control of local matters has been assumed to be normal and beneficial when in fact, in the light of all previous experience it is both abnormal and dangerous.

Surrealism

Not least of the difficulties we confront here is the positively surreal mindframe that modern mass advertising has helped to create. Many millions of people firmly believe that it is perfectly normal to drive a car on a daily basis, or fly on holiday jaunts around the world; that they can enjoy good health when for half or more of them their daily diet consists of denatured, devitalised and demineralised products of chemical laboratories; that their lives can be sustained by factory processed stuffs devoid of the essential vitalities of life. They see nothing odd that manufacturers market packets of cigarettes on which they themselves warn purchasers that 'smoking kills'; that constant discussion is abroad on how to fund the needs of an ever-expanding 'health' service with no attempt made to tax the deleterious salt or sugar based edibles that crowd supermarket shelves; that it is normal to purchase food items flown in from the other side of the world whilst local farms and market gardens which are fully capable of producing them are driven by tax policies and supermarket monopolies into bankruptcy. People who oppose the Europlot are described as right wing extremists as though anything could be more extreme than wholesale attempts to snuff out the national identities of Europe's varied national peoples. It is accepted as normal to hold every year 'arms fairs' where governments can place orders for weapons capable of wiping out entire populations; and that it is normal for every government in our world to pursue energetically a policy of infinite economic expansion. That it is normal for *daily* newspapers to be printed by the million with 80 to 400 pages, for the powerful medium of TV determining the lives and the values of entire societies not to be controlled by society's own educators, philosophers, artists and writers, but subject to the moral imperialism of market forces.

One could expand this tragic catalogue of surrealist phenomena created by over-large and over-centralised government and giant market forces at enormous length, but what it reveals is an utter lack of control of society's direction based on any explicit moral foundation. So that if we feel impelled to reject the structure of government and other institutions that produces such results, and reject them on the grounds that their size prevents them from producing anything better, even as they continue to go from worse to worse, we are still left with the problem of what workable alternative we can promote.

Already mentioned is the role of regional government and the work of the American bioregional movement, from which can be concluded that what is decisive in determining their value is whether they are products of planned scheming from above or of natural groupings of numerous self-regulating communities from below.

Local Parliaments

Consider the strenuous efforts being made by the promoters of the European scheme to project regions for their own purposes. These purposes are simply to weaken the power and influence of present national governments, they are not intended to increase the power of the regions but to increase the power of Brussels. Any such result can only replicate on a greater scale the problems which already afflict us.

This is the backdrop of our plea for village democracy, for assemblies consisting of local people who will devise their own means of taking local decisions on local matters. Any attempt to establish them will no doubt be strongly resisted by those in whose hands power is now held: it is resistance which will be deployed in a variety of ways. But first, what is it they will be resisting?

These new forms of authority will need to be what are in effect new parliaments, local parliaments, peoples parliaments, nothing less. As a kick-off there is nothing at all to stop any group in any community setting up its own local assembly and distributing offices among themselves. In the nature of things at present much of such activity will seem unreal and involve an element of role-playing, but it would be role-playing with a difference.

Such changes cannot be expected to be implemented overnight; ideas travel at their own pace, time is needed for them to gain acceptance and for people to establish local structures which can cope with the consequence of the breakdown of central authorities' functions. It was the authoritarian Fabians who coined the phrase 'the inevitability of gradualness' and some such element will surely be operative here. But let us not ignore that human affairs are in crisis and that crisis elements are likely to impel some major adjustments very swiftly indeed. A breakdown of food supplies, for example, will necessitate its own emergency measures as a matter of course. Any local governmental role-playing will have as its long term aim to assume for the village assembly real power to make decisions, with proper elections and other procedures that ensure the supremacy of local democracy. The role-playing would involve a powerful element of radical education as members sought to discharge their duties.

It is not difficult to conceive an elected local education officer tackling the present school authorities on what is being taught and how money is being spent. Or on why there is so much emphasis on teaching computer skills but none on how to grow food. On why there is no instruction on the dangers of junk foods and why they are dangerous to good health. On the lack of instruction in hand skills such as carpentry, tailoring, leatherwork and so on.

Another elected member for finance might be making it his/her business to question local banks about the quality of their services, their profit margins and their loan policies; he/she would also be to the forefront in promoting local credit schemes, local pensions and savings banks, and a local currency; whilst a Member for Positive Health would be campaigning local doctors to promote fresh, organic food, and sound dietary practice.

The embryo assembly would be constantly concerned to educate by example as well as precept how a new order of local control of local power would operate and in what ways local power could be established and entrenched. Not least it would become a beacon of light and hope against a backdrop of ever deepening crisis, where the likelihood of a collapse of centralised controls is not just a remote possibility, but an event already beginning to unfold.

A Changing World

A world confronted with rapidly rising oil prices, rapidly increasing armament programmes, rapidly increasing human numbers, rapidly increasing consolidation of economic and fiscal power on a global scale, rapidly increasing disease and epidemic outbreaks, rapidly increasing dangers to food and water supplies, combined with a rapidly increasing collapse of natural life-support systems and the mounting effects of global warming, is a world of constantly increasing danger. When one adds to this the current backdrop of mounting fears, tensions, phobias, paranoia's and hysterias related to what is called 'terrorism', even though more American citizens annually kill more of each other than those killed beyond its borders, that danger is being inflated to a degree of irrationality for which sane people will be wise to take their own precautionary measures while there is time.

Any one or more of the above factors is capable of engendering a global economic collapse and it is no more than ordinary caution to seek to establish some at least of the elements of safe measures in anticipation of its outcome. Widespread unemployment, the collapse of any resources to fund welfare or relief programmes to mitigate hunger and homelessness, are not the basis on which democratic values of freedom, justice, tolerance and the due process of law can comfortably flourish.

What is likely to ensue from this impending economic and social collapse is more anger, duly cultivated by one species or another of mob oratory. Such utterance may be counted on to seek to pinpoint one minority or another, or several together, as being the causes of the tribulations people are enduring. Some kind of centralised form of mob rule on a mass basis will doubtless be 'democratically' elected to power, after which no dissenting minority of race, religion or radical opinion will be safe as a new era of persecution, arbitrary rule and war-making erupts.

Statesmanship

'The supreme function of statesmanship is to provide against preventable ills.' Thus Enoch Powell, a former cabinet minister towards the end of his life. Where today is the statesmanship? Where is the ordinary caution and concern to halt this monstrous march of human affairs towards the destiny of damnation that now stares mankind in the face? Where is the governmental policy to halt and reverse the current insane quest for 'growth', to reduce oil consumption and to conserve remaining stocks, to lower the pressure of the global bubble of economic development before it bursts, to cut back on the kind of consumerist profligacy which raises no eyebrows at 400 page newspapers? Where is the collective wisdom to halt the perils of increasing disease-proneness of crops and livestock from industrialised farming and to restore the ordinary sanity of organic principles? Where is there any real collective will to halt carbon emissions which have already given a head start to the melting of polar ice caps and to global warming?

Where is the statesmanship which seeks to educate people on the multiple dangers into which they are running with their passive willingness to embrace an artificially inflated consumerist lifestyle?

When a screaming infant seeks to throw everything out of the pram it may be difficult to predict what will hit the ground first. In our current turmoil the likelihood of the first catastrophe to erupt to be another world war must be very high. Where is the statesmanship to curb or control armament production, so that resources now squandered on it and other war preparations can be diverted to the needs for elementary provisions of food and shelter of millions in want? Or diverted to the great world of culture in all its wonder? Or diverted to the fathomless mysteries of space, time and micro-cellular phenomena?

Such questions raise all the problems, but perhaps the most press-ing question they provoke within the concept presented here is: Can we assume that localised power will behave any more sensibly than when deployed on a mass basis?

We can draw assurance from one key aspect of mass arrange-ments in that its leaders are operating under kinds of compulsion which are far more onerous than the pressures operating locally. As indicated earlier, the pressures on a leader of a centralised mass body *compel* him to act in response to them at the price of ceasing to be a leader at all if he fails to do so. He is not after all, only the leader of a government, but also the leader of a party, and more particularly of a party machine.

The machine exists primarily to gain power, and having once gained it to retain it. We live today in the grip of widely accepted consumerist values and the fruits of power tend to be awarded to those most likely to gratify the appetites embodied in those values; hence the leader dare not pursue policies which will fail to do so. In terms of social cohesion, ecological sanity, the well-being of future generations, and of moral integrity, the transient phenomena of mass motoring and mass air travel are globally destructive almost beyond the power of any words to convey, but what political leader who has won his position on the basis of mass electoral approval and the frenzied backing of his supporters and of the party machine, dare oppose it? He is in the grip of the values promoted assiduously through tabloids, TV and other channels he dare not defy without losing office.

Again, it would be ever so nice to assume that the party machine is financed by the generous contributions of loyal individual party members, but to do so is to overlook not only the rapidly declining membership of these mass parties but the substantial sums fre-quently donated by wealthy business elements. They are backing this particular horse to win on the understanding, even perhaps the assurance, that when the spoils of victory are collected they will be rewarded with their due share in the form of policies that protect and promote their interests. Why otherwise are their contributions made?

The Moral Problem

'Your butcher,' Adam Smith declared two centuries ago, 'does not give you your Sunday joint because he loves you.' and it helps to indicate that the precise moral framework on which economic activity within the social order needs to be conducted is one of those problems for which society has yet to find a clear answer.

It is a problem which is quite irrelevant in any case to the concerns of any mass party leader. In the exercise of such leadership-power there always arises a conflict between the imperatives of moral principle and exigencies of gaining and holding power itself. If the mass electorate has been conditioned by the prostitution of powerful educational forces, such as television, which mount a ceaseless barrage of propaganda to persuade it of the unparalleled allurements of car ownership, air travel, devitalised meat and vegetable factory products as food, of the inevitability of economic 'growth', of the imperative necessity of becoming a member of EUrope (or of 'China', 'America', 'India' or any other ungovernable federal empire), what mass leader seeking to attain or retain power can hope to achieve his aims if they involve speaking out against them?

His bond with the electorate is a power bond, not a moral one, however much he may find it of assistance in his power quest to adumbrate his adherence to high moral principles and however much cherry-picking is involved in selecting them. But if in the tally the quest for economic growth as currently pursued is an evil of measureless dimensions, yet he must pursue it if he is to hold on to power. It is this imperative element of compulsion in a mass leader's position so many would-be reformers seem so tragically content to ignore; they assume that if they can campaign and protest strongly enough on any particular abuse, such as airport development, motorway building, GM crops, Third World debt, the EUroplot, war and armaments, campaigns and protests mounted on the basis of quite impeccable moral principles, they will somehow win the day and the leader will either change course or be replaced.

They overlook the abuses on which they are campaigning are for the most part what is called 'single issues', and such issues are almost invariably the deep concern only of a minority. But the leader to remain leader must serve the majority, however much its mind-frame and off-the-cuff opinion are warped, twisted and poisoned by non-stop consumerist propaganda in the guise of advertising and the general flow of commercialised tendentiousness. And behind the advertising programmes are the boardroom people and not least the big donors to party funds which enable his leadership bid to be financed at all.

In this context we need to note how the grip of advertising values on the mass mind and on social consciousness generally is so all-embracing and so compelling and pervasive that even the voice of the Church, which might be expected to give a moral lead to the general direction of the social order and the general quality of social life, is effectively silenced.

How many pulpit orators dare inveigh against the social evil of mass motoring when the vehicles of most of their listeners habitually crowd the environments of most places of worship during services? Or against mass air travel? Or against the moronic effects of commercial television? Or against the cultural squalor of most television or radio programmes? Or against the socially disruptive and destructive effects of giant supermarkets which have already bankrupted hundreds of thousands of family-owned village shops and driven thousands of small farmers to the wall?

Most of these evils are only a consequential effect of personal choice; their primary source is the power of giant advertising campaigns. Few individuals have either the knowledge or the awareness that might enable them to resist this highly professionalised assault on the frailty of their moral propensities; even fewer of them are ordained ministers, and how many theological training centres are equipped to give instruction on the moral implications of the political and economic evils that now confront us?

These evils of our time stem from the assumptions and the values on which the everyday workings of our economic operations and our political institutions are based, but clergy training rarely provides students with the means to grapple with them. Distinctions between good and evil in these spheres are rarely established and generally blurred into endless depths of ambiguity when they are not altogether ignored.

Hence all too often clergy do not, often because they cannot, give a lead to their flock on the rampant environmental destruction (God's handwork) that our modern lifestyle promotes. Their consciousness tends to be imbued with the same values as those of their flock, so that far from being leaders, all too often they are often passive followers, ensuring that the moral force of religion is side-lined into less consequential matters. Much safer to dwell on personal failings, on matters of sex, family breakdown, divorce, infidelity, or on biblical stories which steer clear of 'controversy' or involvement in 'politics'.

Community Morality

It is of course part of the legacy of mass government that the word 'political' has come to carry its own apparently dubious moral overtones so that it may be pertinent to ask would things be any different in our parish assemblies? In such a local context the bond between the leaders and the led is only secondarily a power bond; it is primarily personal, a bond in consequence on which moral judgements will have their own play of force. We have argued that these personal bonds are the strongest force in determining a community's identity — but this is just not true of national government, where the strongest forces operating on it are the economic and political ambitions of minority leadership groups, with their concomitant greed for money and power. It is after all precisely these forces that are shaping modern states, ugly, violent, impersonal, ruthless, materialist and with the ecological morals of an alley cat. Their leaders can afford to ignore moral considerations; the working of modern economic systems they presume to oversee is based indeed on their rejection, and the disposition of power in mass societies is such that any leaders seeking to heed moral prescription are simply replaced by others who ignore them. What political leader in the climate of current inflated consumerist propensities who advocated government expenditure on motorways should be diverted to boosting family organic farms, or that a heavy tax on air and road transport should finance a massive subsidy on rail travel, could hope to survive?

The local community leader is operating within a quite different context. He is the neighbour of the people who have elected him; he is dependent for his position on their personal judgement and their approval; his office is within their effective reach, he either conforms to their moral verdicts or he is out. Private donations from wealthy backers cannot help him if his neighbours disapprove of his policies or his personality; there is no party machine other than that controlled by them to operate between the electorate and the elected, and no amount of spin by the local newspaper can decide his fate. He is elected because his neighbours think he is worthy to be elected; just that.

It does not follow that the play of local forces cannot at times reflect the negative aspects of the human disposition. A local landowner, if elected, will not always be averse to voting for a highway development which will enhance the value of his property; two or three malcontents are well able to poison the quality of community relationships with all the bitterness and bile of which they are capable; whispering campaigns involving grievous degrees of character assassination are not altogether unknown in village or parish communities; hostilities, even hatreds, can become rife with no apparent acceptable reason, and so on. But other factors are also at work in a community which are apt scarcely to be seen or heard in the play of national power games.

Even today, for example, despite the awesome degree with which national political forces presume to run local community affairs, despite the disappearance of local family-owned shops as supermarkets proliferate, even despite *national* policies over such essentially local matters as schools, hospitals and surgeries, planning, transport, and other matters, there is still quite astonishing degree of freely given service active in many voluntary organisations in many communities. A whole range of sports, football, cricket, bowls, darts, tennis, rugby or snooker, will be run by the duly elected officers of their organisations; there will be local bodies to care for the aged, the housebound, for invalids, for pets, for the bereaved, for the local war memorial and so on. Local charities, Dogs for the Blind, Children in Need, the RSPCA, The British Legion, Dr Barnardo's, Fair Trade, the NSPCC, these will be up and running in addition to numerous local church and political bodies, to village trusts, a carnival committee and so on. All part of the warp and woof of local life, all indicating the flames of altruism and the desire to give disinterested service are brightly burning. What will happen when the spirit of democracy comes alive and becomes fully operative in their affairs? What *can* happen but a surge of genuine social health and well-being where excess and single-minded pursuit of anti-social objectives such as 'growth' at any price and at the cost of vital community relationships are rejected for a spirit of service and concern for the public weal as a first priority?

Bureaucratic Cost

A local assembly, as well as being infinitely more democratic would make for infinitely less expensive ways of providing local services. The current towering superstructure of bureaucratic administration now required to run national schemes for health, for education, welfare and other matters would simply disappear. At present a quite disproportionate amount of budgetary provision goes simply on the costs of administration. In the UK we now have more hospital administrators than we have hospital beds.

A further factor here is the role of drugs and drug companies in a national service. One medical authority has declared that 'In Europe and the USA the drug companies now control the medical profession. To a large extent doctors have become the marketing arms of the pharmaceutical industry.'[1] The same author asserts many widely used drugs are dangerous and often do more harm than healing.

What stands out is that most drugs are excessively overpriced and that their cost, as well as the costs of medical equipment and mundane ancillary items such as bandages, play a quite disproportionate role in health care budgets. A local health service would be free to break out of the current constraints imposed by giant drug companies. Local labour could be employed to make equipment and such items as bandages at a fraction of the prevailing charges, and the way would also be open to employ natural traditional remedies from local services such as herb gardens.

There is a pronounced tendency to dismiss remedies based on natural ingredients as being so much hocus pocus; it is an attitude which ignores how much more hocus pocus there is in the promotion of high powered products of the giant pharmaceutical companies. The size of their advertising budgets is a key pointer here; the whole emphasis of the industry is not on healing but in making money, often in ways which are none too scrupulous with regard to the long term effects of repeated use.

What is noticeable about a national service is its disregard of positive health promotion. It is really a National Sickness service. Very few people have any detailed understanding of how their bodies work and are generally ignorant of the needs of their respiratory, digestive, excretory and other organs; it is this ignorance which enables advertisers to persuade them to purchase highly flavoured, devitalised and chemicalised items masquerading as food on such a regular basis as to make one form of ill health or another inevitable. Most of the shelves in most food stores today are institutionalised assaults on any attempt to provide a proper health service; a locally run service would be aware of the relationship between this factor and the effect on its health budget and be concerned to promote locally-produced chemical-free food and to make people aware of the true conditions of bodily health. Helping people to understand you cannot buy good health, you can only live it, and a genuinely

---

[1]   Vernon Coleman: *How To Stop Your Doctor Killing You*, 2nd Ed. p. 244.

democratic local health authority would be a front runner in promoting the ways decent health can be attained.

It may well be asserted, indeed it frequently is, that village people are apt to make mistakes with their limited knowledge and that these can carry a heavy cost in terms of both money and resources, mistakes which experts with their greater knowledge can avoid. This of course is only too true. Inadequate supervision of local building operations may prompt a contractor to install drainage pipes of smaller than specified dimensions, or to use sub-standard construction materials and so on, practices which only come to light after a lapse of time and when invoices have been finally processed.

Perhaps we should bear in mind that no system of government can ever be perfect, if only because it presumes a perfection of human nature that would bore any such entity on which it operated into extinction. More to the point is to take on board the sheer magnitude of the 'mistakes' that seem to stem from centralised governments as a matter of course.

The UK government has for decades pursued a policy of giant hospitals; this has involved the closure of numerous cottage hospitals formerly frequently run by local voluntary committees on the basis of local fund-raising efforts. The new giant institutions, if only because of the much wider area they serve, involving lengthy journeys, either by private vehicles or public transport. This holds true not only for patients, whose treatment involves repeated attendance, but for friends and relatives who may wish to visit long-stay patients. It also holds true for the thousands of doctors, nurses and ancillary staff who work in them. We are here seeing again how expert knowledge plus technical considerations are presumed to dominate purely human factors. Only one large centre, it is assumed will be able to provide all the elaborate technical equipment and expertise available to cope with the deleterious effects of modern chemicalised lifestyles on human bodies.

What is ignored here is any radical assessment of the causes of so much modern ill-health, often expressed in increasingly subtle and tragic forms and for which they pose problems about the lifestyle rather than the treatment. Nevertheless the policy of vast hospital structures remote from many peoples homes persists, the cost of the administration soars,[2] and despite the best efforts of doctors and

---

[2] In 1997 administrative costs stood at £2,150 million and by 2001 had reached £2,625 million whilst overall per capita costs has risen in 2001 from £951.36 to £1,200.57 in 2003.

nurses, the service appears to be imploding into even longer waiting periods for treatment. People today are not healthier because of the health service, they are more in need of treatment because of conceptual defects in its purposes, its structures and its operation. It is said that prevention is better than cure, but who is concerned with prevention? Perhaps it is the health service that is sick.

And what are we to say of our schools and an education service run by centralised bureaucrats, with their national targets and budgets, their huge schools and their declining standards? It is not only that after a generation or more of such misconceived efforts more than a fifth of pupils leaving school are now judged to be functionally non-literate, such an approach ignores quite fundamental considerations of freedom and the inevitable conflict of interest between any form of governmental power exercised on such a scale and the concerns of the governed. It involves concerns about the rights, and indeed the freedom, of parents to determine how and why their children should be educated, a concern to acknowledge that children are first and foremost the responsibility of their parents rather than of any government ministry, that any surrender of such responsibility to governmental power structures involves an abandonment of moral obligation and a surrender to forces beyond any prospect of moral assessment or control. It involves indeed whether children are to be educated in terms of parental morality and judgement, or whether they are to be educated to slot in with the power-oriented needs of centralised structures.

Nevertheless the concept of centralised control of this vital aspect of community life continues to dominate the political scene and with it its absurd policy of giant schools. It is a policy which we cannot fail to relate to its consequences. Modern schools, whatever successes they may register in examination results for a minority, (itself a highly questionable standard), are producing a generation of hooligans, social failures and misfits. The evidence is all around us. A Chief constable warns us we are confronted with bands of feral youths in our urban centres whose members have no regard for moral distinction or for law and order.

An American conference of mostly professional youth specialists in 2004 looked at some of the problems; problems not unlike those afflicting young people in many developed (are they perhaps over-developed?) countries. The problems involve violence, depression, drugs, alcohol abuse, anti-social pursuits, suicide and much else of adverse nature now on the increase.

They entitled their gathering 'The Crisis of American Youth', although it could well have related to the crisis of youth over a far wider field. And their conclusions? They were unanimous that one major cause was that their schools were too large.

It might be thought that the experts and the professionals who run things from their huge central controlling structure would have sat up and taken notice of such a conclusion and modified their policies, even perhaps making a U-turn and promoting small rather than large schools.

Such thinking ignores the natural inbuilt resistances to any kind of change that involves a diminution, or an increased difficulty in administering, of power. The giant schools policy continues so that, regardless of the consequences, thousands of youngsters are daily transported from their own home areas to attend and then regardless of the school timetable, and the way any extra-curricular activities become in large measure determined by bus schedules, bussed out again.

The American conference was insistent that in creating difficulties in establishing relationships or a sense of belonging, in diffusing the sense of relatedness to a common focus of emotional regard, in promoting a gang warfare culture and a general contempt for authority or decent social standards, overlarge schools were a highly significant factor in the general malaise of American youth.

Inevitably we are dealing here with a diversity of behaviour symptoms within a social and environmental structure redolent with its own complexities, we are, we may say, dealing with a range of varying emotional promptings and responses on which general trends rather than hard and fast conclusions may be drawn. We are not in the world of mathematical equations but of human behaviour, one where professional experience and competence allied to statistical and other evidence, can do no more than establish signposts of where current trends are likely to lead us.

Chapter Six

Resolving the Problem of War

Localised control of resources. – Unequal members of federations lead to domination by the most powerful. – UN peace a daydream. – Multiplicity of countries reduces risk of major war. – The 'Truce of God'. – Medieval war was an outlet for aggression, modern war much less so but more destructive. – Local power emphasises morality, giant power emphasises power. – Influence of TV – Local communities to have reps on TV, radio and mass newspaper boards. – Outlaw armament production. – Lesson of Iraq war. – Aggression in male psyche. – Swiss example of peace. Is it based on costing 'prosperity? – Contrary trends to localisation and giantism. – 19th Century concepts of centralised statehood dominate Arab Israel conflict. – Democracy involves citizen involvement.

If local communities have their hands on local resources the mere talk of a national government seeking to start a war will run into its own difficulties. All the guns and planes in the world are not much use without food and transport services. So, in the cause of peace, we can anticipate nothing less than the globalisation of localisation. In the long run it is doubtful if global peace can be secured in any other way. Current assumptions about securing peace are riddled with impracticabilities and unrealities. Currently there is a persistent belief that a vast unicellular, supranational authority, with sufficient military clout to enforce peace everywhere, will need to be established. It is a concept which runs into all the problems discussed here. Who would control such a body? How could it fail to become the catspaw of global multinational corporations? Could is possibly coexist with democracy and freedom, given too that any such authority would inevitably be beyond the capacity of the citizen body to control it on a democratic basis?

Current thinking in any case takes no account of an essential prerequisite for the successful working of any federation. History is eloquent that if the members of a federation are significantly unequal in size and strength it will only be a matter of time before the bigger members dominate it. This proved the case in 'Germany', which, after its formation by Bismark, soon became dominated by Prussia and in the USSR, which was dominated by Russia. What ensues is not so much a federation as an empire under the dominance of the most powerful member. It is noticeable that in the USA and in Switzerland, two of the most successful federations in the record, no single member is strong enough to dominate the rest. This does not of course resolve the problem of the power drives of any federation when it gets big enough to dominate other federations, as the USA does today. We can anticipate the prospect of China, or India, achieving a degree of power to rival that of the USA, especially when the power of the latter inevitably declines. But this does not resolve the problem of war so much as open up the prospect of even bigger global wars between rival federations. Hence any projects for a world federation will need to involve a massive scaling down of the big powers that now dominate world affairs so that the members achieve some approximation of parity in terms of size and strength.

The same power cannot be in two places at the same time; either people have power in their hands or they don't. Either giant governments and corporations have it in their hands or they haven't. Nevertheless the dream of some such international authority continues to shine like a beacon in the eyes of many pacifists and peace lovers, as well as being vaguely acknowledged as a good thing by a great many other people. The fact is that they have no grasp at all of the power realities involved or that any such body would be only too to likely make peace-lovers and their ideals its first victims. But then, an anxious enquiring voice will be heard to venture, 'Won't largely self-governing local communities or bioregional provinces sometimes want to make war on other neighbouring communities?'

Perhaps they will, but what would such wars be about? And how indeed would they be fought? Such an event was commonplace in medieval Europe, just as it was in the Jewish tribal wars of ancient Palestine, which feature so prominently in the Old Testament. Indeed it may be salutary to be reminded that much of the Old Testament is the propagandistic accounts of these wars by the winners, which may well account for the bloodthirsty revenges and retributions that are described, as distinct from the actualities of the events. How would the record read if written by the losers? In any case any view of such wars may need to be hedged about with an understanding of the social and moral beliefs of the time, and buttressed too by an awareness that in medieval Europe, as doubtless in ancient Palestine, whilst a war may well have been always going on somewhere, the fact remains, as Professor Leopold Kohr pertinently observes, 'somewhere is not the same as everywhere.' Kohr also points out that the mere multiplicity of borders was an important factor in limiting the spread and scale of wars. How indeed could it not be? But he also draws attention to another limitation, one called 'The Truce of God',

> The Middle Ages enjoyed such relatively numerous periods of peace not only by making peace and war divisible in *space* as a result of the boundary-ridden small-state system. With a true touch of genius, they made them divisible also *in time*. Their leaders never believed in the unattainable nonsense of an eternal peace, and therefore never wasted their energy in trying to establish it. Knowing the substance of which man was made, they wisely based their systems on his shortcomings, not his pretensions. Unable to prevent war, they did the next best thing. They tried to control it. And in this they succeeded signally through an institution which they called *Treuga Dei*, the *Truce of God*.
>
> This truce was based on the concept that war, as it was divisible regionally, was divisible also into separate actions and periods. According to its original provisions, all warfare had to be interrupted on Saturday noon and could not be resumed until Monday morning in order to ensure the undisturbed worship of the Lord on Sunday. Subsequently, the period of truce was extended to include Thursday in honour of Christ's ascension, Friday in reverent commemoration of the crucifixion, and all of Saturday in memory of His entombment. In addition to these time limitations, a number of places were declared immune from military action. Thus, even in the midst of war, neither churches and churchyards, nor fields at harvest time could be made the scene of battle. Finally, entire groups of persons such as women, children, old people, or farmers working in fields were placed under a special protection and had to be left unmolested. Infractions of the Truce of God were punished by the Church as well as the State, and particularly severe violations with long years of exile in Jerusalem.[1]

Perhaps the same author is also right in assuming that human nature being what it is there will always be wars, but in that case it is clear that medieval wars provided for the maximum outlets for aggression for those who wished to fight with the minimum degrees of

---

[1] *The Breakdown of Nations*, Leopold Kohr. 2001 Edition by Green Books in association with New European Publications, pp. 78–82

social damage; whereas modern wars, with their long-range techno-logical emphasis on bombers and rockets, would appear to do the reverse. It is one thing to satisfy aggressive instincts by knocking an enemy fighter from his horse, and perhaps later collecting a ransom from a prisoner, but what aggressive outlet is provided to an airman half a mile in the air who in pressing a bomb-release button destroys half a city?

Advertising Power

What is also missing today is a quality of mercy much in evidence in medieval Europe, but which today seems to play scarcely any part at all in modern warfare. How many German prisoners died at Stalin-grad? How many Russians died in the fighting? How many Viet-namese peasant families were fatally poisoned with the thousands of defoliation bombs dropped on their luckless country by US bomb-ers? Who knows? Who now even cares? Yet we regard our forbears as being backward and we term the era in which they lived com-pared with our own as 'the dark ages'.

The question would appear to be not whether the political or eco-nomic empowerment of local parishes today would be any better than our present arrangements, but whether they could possibly be worse? Clearly they would have some difficulty in being so, but the focus on medieval warfare brings to the fore another factor alto-gether absent in the modern era which was a potent reality in former times. Dare one even refer to moral leadership?

Where, one may well ask, is it today? The fact that in an empow-ered parish business would be based very much more on the moral quality of personal relationships, rather than on power relationships which empower central controlling organs at the expense of the indi-vidual; this suggests that the important function of moral appraisal and determination would be a factor to be reckoned with and could not easily be dismissed out of hand. The supposition that the grosser aspects of the human disposition will always prevail regardless, ignores that whereas in a giant mass society it prevails because powerful economic and political forces have an interest in ensuring its dominance and can always swamp the still, small voice of reason and conscience; this is not the case in empowered communities, since in such entities relationships matter, hence so will morality. Since relationships are by definition determinative, so too is moral-ity. The moral factor becomes determinative for yet another reason; the people who are apt to seek to generate public concern and alert others to the danger or nefariousness of a particular course or decision generally constitute a minority, often a very small one. By and large in matters of public policy most people most of the time tend to be passive, or even acquiescent. They have a ready disposition to trust those in public office and to assume that they generally act for the best. This remains true despite the no less general attitude of cynicism about the motives of those in office. In huge mass societies the voice of minority moral concern over any issue is all to apt to be swamped by matters engaging the majority, matters apt to centre on immediate concerns related to pockets and stomachs, to say nothing of sex, rather than to long-term consequences of current decisions, or to abstract considerations such as truth, justice, sanity or peace. All of this simply helps to underline that since a mass body is one dominated in its governance by power considerations, and that since a self-regulating local community is dominated by personal relationships, it follows that the moral factors of those relationships will be stronger in the community than the same factors in a huge mass.

In this context we have to face that any such evaluation has to be subject to other factors when the self-regulating force of a community is undermined by outside forces. This is noticeably true of the way consumerist or boardroom propaganda via TV and tabloids, to say nothing of papers and journals seeking to cater for the professional and possibly educated classes, dominates public consciousness. All the morally alert spirits in any community today are hard put to prevail against this propaganda, more money is spent on it today than the government spends on education. How can the values of culture, history, moral wisdom, tradition or ecological sanity hope to prevail in any community given the prevailing distribution of this propaganda power?

What is the answer here? Do we pass laws against such advertising, and throw the baby of freedom out with the bathwater of state regulation? Do we seek to persuade people to ignore a message which is inflicted on their attention at almost every turn of their working day? Or do we assert the right of each local community to have representative members on the relevant governing bodies, of TV, radio and mass newspapers and journalists. The present practice is of course an effective denial of this right.

Simply to pose such questions brings us face to face with how the complexities of modern technologies are battering at basic concepts of localised freedom and independence. It is possible today for powerful means of propaganda, of misinformation and the promotion of mass phobias, hysterias, animosities, war fevers and violence, to say nothing of pornographic programmes which are an affront to human dignity, can be transmitted globally from a single centre.

Human moral consciousness, once the fruit of family and community relationships, of teaching in local schools and churches, so that its picture of the wider world, however mistaken was only a marginal factor of the whole, is now at the mercy and being vigorously assailed by giant commercial forces concerned only to impinge on that consciousness for purely commercial ends regardless of any degree of human degradation involved.

This is only one of many problems that a focus on scale as a primary political factor brings to the fore, indicating the enormity of the transformation of mindframe and practical policy objectives we need to make. It may also indicate the extent of our need for high level academic engagement, a need, because it is so obviously being so ill met that it betokens a lack of awareness even of the extent of our need.

Universities were once centres for the pursuit of wisdom; this was indeed their raison d'être, today they are centres of careerology; the higher the exam results the better the job prospects. This wholesale switch of functions from a pursuit which might soar above the everyday needs of society to take a deeper and more profound view of what society was and where it might be going, to a mundane concern for jobs and careers is surely a marked feature of a civilisation in decline. Nothing is more urgent today than to recover the university role of the search for wisdom and understanding unfettered by the power of the state and of market forces..

War Versus Local Democracy

These general considerations barely touch on the crude imperatives of violence, armaments and war as they prevail in the modern world. There are already doubtless enough war weapons in the world which could make it uninhabitable, so that the immediate problem is one of controlling their production and controlling their use. On this it is not difficult to envisage regional or continental peace brigades having the power to search for and destroy stockpiles of military hardware, to buffer attempts by rogue states to spread by conquest, and committed by a special Peace Charter to use non-violent means wherever possible. It would be manned by volunteers, perhaps as a graduation exercise to citizenship status by young men and women, and controlled and funded through elected government diplomats.

It goes, one would like to think, without saying, that all armament production by private entrepreneurs would be outlawed. The problem then arises, how to prevent war when a government is bent on waging it? Immediately one is confronted with the contingent problem of promoting or maintaining democratic rule. How many democratically elected governments want to wage war?

In present conditions of mass, centrally controlled governments, quite a lot, even if many of their citizens are opposed to war. This problem surfaced in 2003 when the British and American governments decided to invade Iraq. Millions of people protested in street parades around the world, but to no avail and the war went ahead. What is of note here is that political leaders in both countries were able to secure legislative compliance with their policy decisions on grounds which have since proved to be quite false. They argued that Iraq's rulers were an immediate threat to their security because they possessed powerful weapons of mass destruction. In the event the Iraq government and its forces collapsed like a pack of cards and no WMD's were ever found because they did not exist.

What is the lesson here? That on a mass basis democracy does not work? That elected representatives can be bullied, cajoled and deceived into supporting war and that leaders can remain in power even after instigating a war which has no justification? Simply to say as much is to convey the enormity of the problem. If, in both countries, locally empowered democracy had prevailed, if local people, instead of joining street demonstrations, had organised the cessation of rail and bus services, disrupted communications, blocked the ports, promoted a barrage of opposition through *their* TV and radio station, *their* newspapers and media outlets, neither government could have embarked on aggression. They would not even have attempted to do so!

But we do not, yet, live in a world of empowered local communities and in future, as some countries will achieve that status, others won't, there is obviously going to be a prolonged period before effective democracy becomes globally operative. It will be a period of considerable danger of full-scale war, even as it provides us with an added incentive to make democracy globally effective with all possible speed.

Beyond all this is there not an element in the human psyche, perhaps the male psyche, which is innately aggressive and war prone?

An element which ensures that radical or religious rivalries will always be vicious and bloody? Perhaps there is, but need it always be so virulent? Or dominant?

In chapter 3 reference was made to the success of Switzerland in achieving considerable prosperity and a prolonged period of peace despite the extent to which it incorporates within its borders emphatic divisions of race, religion and language. Yet it was noted how these same factors have helped to provoke repeated major wars in countries on its borders. Given the success of the Swiss solution to the problem of war could its system be more generally applied?

War and Economics

There is no doubt that geography has been the main reason for the endurance of the Swiss small-scale, cantonal system. When whole valleys are cut off from others by alpine snows and formidable heights, people tend to get on with the business of getting a decent living from a harsh natural terrain rather than fostering animosities and planning to wage war. To this we should add the factor of affluence itself. Prosperity tends to make people peaceful whereas poverty tends to make them pugnacious and Swiss prosperity has ensued from successfully riding the crest of a wave of economic expansion which has swept across many parts of the world. It is a wave still having considerable momentum, but will it last?

There are a number of ominous factors in the equation suggesting it won't and that it could end abruptly and even catastrophically. Will a poverty-stricken Switzerland, with bankrupt banks and a widespread collapse of the international trade that sustains it, be as pacific as when prosperous?

We can only leave the question open, because attempts to answer it beg a great many other questions related to resources, sustainable lifestyles and the increasing globalisation of investment economics. Here it needs to be stressed that the Swiss system, based on small, largely independent Cantons, governed in turn on strong democratic principles, really does work. It does achieve stability, prosperity and peaceful coexistence; but can it be applied to danger spots in other parts of the world?

One answer is that everywhere attempts are already being made to do so, and in some measure successfully. Successfully in the case of what was formerly designated Czechoslovakia and Yugoslavia, but even peacefully and contentedly in the case of Latvia, Estonia and Lithuania, which have regained their independence from the former USSR.

Indeed, all over the world we may note this curious contradiction of purposeful moves in one direction, for fragmentation and the assertion of independent nationhood of small ethnic identities stemming from the aspirations of local people, opposing well financed (at taxpayer's expense) campaigns from the top for forms of unity which are inherently bogus, such as one based in Brussels.

But the question naturally arises, can the plea for small nationhood be reconciled with the aspirations of opposed ethnic or religious peoples, especially if their relationships are already embittered by repeated outbreaks of violence and killing? The answer must surely be, why not give the Swiss solutions a chance? Nothing is certain in such situations except the certainty of more violence if attempts to resolve it fail.

Israel and The Arabs

The Arab/Israel conflict is a case in point. Both sides appear to be trapped in rival concepts of 19th century statehood, concepts which are rigid, inflexible and can only produce ever more violence until one side or other is overwhelmingly defeated. The Israelis, haunted by the harrowing experience of the holocaust in Nazi Germany, are adamant on the need for a unified, centralised Israeli state. In this they are pursuing policies which can only increase Arab antagonism and hatred. They appear to be basing their attitude to the Arab world on their concept of the Old Testament as being some sort of land registry, an attitude which of course makes a conflict with Palestinian people as inevitable as a sunrise.

So the Israelis are building a gigantic defensive wall in an attempt physically to isolate themselves from the surrounding Arab countries. For a number of reasons it will not work, not least because of the extent to which the Israeli economy is dependent on Palestinian labour. But the wall represents too a failure of the imagination, a failure to devise a solution based on a need to live together rather than one accepting the inevitability of chronic hostility. If, after all, the cantonal principle works in Switzerland why should it not work in Israel? If two or three large Palestinian towns or cities were granted semi-independence within a Palestinian/Israeli Confederation their occupants would at once become ardent protectors of their new status; any attempt to destroy them as part of Israel by other Arabs would be fiercely resisted. Both Palestinians and Israelis would gain from the new concord and there would be no losers![2]

And why should the same approach not be adopted wherever territorial rivalry prevails the world over? A marked feature of those areas of the world until recently under colonial rule shows a large number of frontiers which are straight lines on maps. Indeed the straight line is almost the logo of colonialism; they have been drawn by empire builders with little regard for the tribal or ethnic realities of the peoples whose territory has been so arbitrarily designated. At some stage, if the world is ever to know peace, they will need to be redrawn to accord with the boundaries of the lands on which local people live.

The Problem of Violence

The world is already in turmoil from a failure to recognise and apply these considerations, but it will be clear that in themselves they can only be part of any solution to the problem of how to outlaw organised warfare from human affairs. The global turmoil is in part a product of several other factors such as excessive human numbers, the stranglehold on public affairs exercised by giant commercial interests, the extent to which those same interests are stripping the world of its irreplaceable rain-forest cover, the promotion of levels of consumption of industrialised products which are destroying its remaining reserves of finite resources and helping to promote the meltdown of the polar icefields.

All this and a great deal more is contributing to another, and perhaps decisive, factor in the equation. The human home on this planet has always been, from prehistoric times, the small tribe or local community. It is the oldest social unit in history and these same dominant commercial forces are achieving a consummation of their profit-driven drives only at the price of its virtual elimination. There is little profound research into the consequences of this appalling transformation, but the available evidence indicates it is largely responsible for the everyday character of the modern world, a world which is ugly, formless, violent, and characterised by every kind and degree of social ill to which a name might be given.

Here we need to focus on violence. In societies described as 'affluent' older people are apt to bewail the behaviour of young people.

---

[2]   This solution was first proposed by Professor Leopold Kohr over 40 years ago in an article in the *San Juan Star* of Puerto Rico, and which was republished in *Fourth World Review* No. 130, 2004.

'Why' to cite their common complaint, 'is their behaviour so anti-social'! And the answer is because there is no longer any definable traditional social structure to which their natural desire to express allegiance might be given. The question of work may be far removed from problems of global war, but this is the price we pay for replacing the old fulfilment in work as master craftsmen of one kind or another with subservient attendance on machines, for the disruption and diminution of family life achieved by television, for the destruction of community relationships as local, family-owned shops are bankrupted by giant super-markets, where instead of neighbours doing business with neighbours, strangers ignore each other.

The forces which have accomplished this are simply murdering civilisation. When the oldies see the young with their autos, their mobiles, T.V., air travel and the rest of it, they moan young people have everything and are not happy. In reality the young have nothing of fundamental value. They have neither the stability nor the security of a vibrant local social structure, their work prospects are insecure and often demeaning, they are aware that the dominant forces determining the quality of their lives do not stem from their own moral decisions but from commercial appetites in the hands of a powerful and largely anonymous minority, a minority utterly beyond any prospect of any kind of moral responsiveness that does not bow to the supreme god of commercial profit. They feel abused in a profound spiritual sense, they feel isolated and alienated and of course they are angry! How could they not be?

But it is this anger which makes them ready recruits for battles on the wider front, wider than the football terraces and the urban no-go-for-the-police-after-dark-centres; the drug and the drink scenarios make them ready recruits for any war against anything or anybody that is on offer. Deep in themselves young people are today without hope, without confidence in the future, without any meaningful life goal; those not complete vegetables are aware they have been betrayed and of course their anger, often hidden even from themselves, is beyond measure.

It is anger which can be hitched to any spout of political discontent, with or without religious overtones, as events in the Arab world at this time are witness. If people are angry and want to wage war there is no power on earth which can restrain them; what needs to be done is to locate the forces which prompt men to fight and to examine how those forces can be diverted into less destructive outlets.

The main matters of contention and war proneness in the world today are land, water, oil and human identity. On the first, that of land, we have already advanced the principle of cantonisation and the delineation of territorial borders to accord with the desires of the people who live on it. The questions of access to oil and water are of course political matters which only democratic practice coupled with a positive application of the principles of justice and equity can hope to ensure a peaceful process in global affairs.

Democracy and Peace

The same is true of human identity. For more than half a century millions of Africans, to take but one tragic example, have been killed, rendered homeless or reduced to destitution as a result of tribal conflict arising from the denial of tribal identities in different parts of that vast continent. Since Macmillan's 'Wind of Change' swept through Africa it has seen 186 coups, 26 wars and the consequential deaths of seven million victims. It is a torment that continues and Africa awaits the advent of some wise, far-seeing statesmen who will grasp the need for a robust affirmation of their tribal realities and roots if peace is ever going to prevail.

We have to recognise that the practice of democracy bestows its own dignity on those who engage it: it is the insistence of many formerly suppressed and colonial peoples across the world in asserting their birthright of a share in that dignity which is shaking our world to its depths. The path to peace involves a total acknowledgement of the justice of their claim.

The issue of democracy is indeed closely bound up with that of peace, for it is mainly through democratic procedures that the (largely) male disposition to aggressive-self-affirmation can be tamed. Democracy means that individual citizens are empowered and that, if they so wish, they can play a positive creative role in the conduct of affairs. Owing to the highly centralised development of the worlds of politics and commerce these roles are accessible only to a tiny minority in 'leadership' positions, themselves all too often puppets of powerful market elements which donate liberally to their 'election' campaigns and manipulate the media message. The vast majority of people are reduced to roles which are passive, acquiescent and conformist, a situation far from being remotely democratic is the very antithesis of democracy. The result is a situation ripe for many kinds of mischief. People, especially men, who live in a social and political framework which denies the significance of their maleness and their creative male powers, are the raw recruiting material for military adventures anywhere, which is why modern armies are manned largely by volunteers and why conscripts are a secondary element.

Democracy involves citizen involvement, not in the shallow terms of marking a ballot paper every few years, but in terms of everyday decision-making in terms of the cut and thrust of power deployment in the local, perhaps tribal, ambience. If power, instead of being centralised, is widely dispersed, fragmented and made responsive to local needs and views it is helping to channel the energies of power away from the abuse of power which creates conflict and war. Dispersed power can create numerous possibilities of human fulfilment. Centralised power is today a major source of human frustration.

Men resort to violence when they are led by corrupt, power-seeking undemocratic leaders, or when they feel driven to desperation by their common lot. There is of course no guarantee that a world of genuinely democratic micro-states will not experience outbreaks of violence somewhere at some time; but, somewhere is not everywhere and sometimes is not always. In any case, however stupid and tragic, small wars are preferable to big wars and the danger today is that big wars are only too likely. The monster forms of power we have so unwisely allowed to develop will erupt in ways which will eventually obliterate even the possibility of any form of organised warfare itself.

Chapter Seven

Mass Communication

Effect of railways and mass newspapers on local power, views replace news. – T.V. a new uncontrollable giant. – How is media power being used? – Government by the people – Power of advertising. – Car ownership. – Oil reserves. – Destruction of citizen moral choice. – Smith's error about market self-regulation. – Absence of democratic media control. – People conditioned to accept alternatives projected to them. – Need to tackle problem on a local basis. – Institutions now have a life of their own. – Secret citizen surveillance now common and extensive. – Need for TV control by non-commercial elements concerned to promote the public interest.

The Local Worldview

Before the railway age people communicated mainly by word of mouth, and mainly with each other. Only a minority of people would travel any great distance beyond their own homes, and the views of others on matters in the wider world could come, when they came at all, from the few who did travel, from public proclamations and such gleanings as might be gathered from the parson and churchgoing.

That view might well be piecemeal and with exaggerations and other distortions as might be retailed according to the disposition of the source. But perhaps such defects did not greatly matter; a man's life would centre on his home, his work and the social life of his local community. It was local events and local relationships which formed the stuff of his worldview and there were limits to the extent to which it might differ from actuality or be distorted.

The railway, and even more the printing press, transformed the whole picture. *Mass* travel and *mass* circulation of newspapers enabled the world to be brought to the door of every home in every village, and with it a picture which was inevitably second-hand and no longer mainly the product of personal observation or experience.

It was a picture increasingly the product of other peoples' views and those people were the ones who edited or controlled the mass readership newspapers. Local discussion was no longer focussed on the views of local people about local events, it became increasingly discussion of other peoples views of other events in other parts, and it was of course indicative of a portentous shift of power away from the locale to centres where finance was available to own or edit mass journals. It became possible on a mass scale to project views as news, and news was often little more than views, but since economic life was still largely based on local farming and local industry there were obvious constraints on the extent to which distortion was possible.

The really important effect of the increasing centralisation of both economic and political institutions seems to have been that, power, in a multitude of forms, was transferred from local to national and even global centres; mass production for mass consumption was accompanied by the virtual emasculation of local government as the state government assumed both the right and the power to ordain local education, health, social welfare and other local matters.

The Media

The ensuing *disempowerment* of local life by these developments was accentuated to an enormous degree by the development of television; it was in fact one of the most portentous transformations of life in human history. Local people ceased to be masters of their own view of life and the world, they became the passive recipients of the view of others, and that view was one arranged for them by others whose interests were anchored to matters having little in common with those of the mass viewer, and arranged with a consummate degree of skill that effectively concealed much of the inevitable bias of the projectors.

It was indeed a new form of power, but power at the price of disempowering the mass viewer. How could it be otherwise?

It is noteworthy that Anthony Sampson, in his 'Anatomy of Britain in the 21st Century' entitled, *Who Runs This Place?*[1] subtitles his chapter on 'Broadcasters': 'Controlling the Uncontrollable'. He also projects a diagrammatic picture of the disposition of power in modern Britain with a number of interlocking circles of varying sizes. Among the smaller circles are the cabinet, Parliament, the Palace and, nearly the smallest of them all, is the political parties. Larger

[1]   *Who Runs This Place?* Anthony Sampson. John Murray 2004 ISBN 0-7195-6564-2

than all four together is a circle denoting the Prime Minister but largest, larger even than the 'Rich', is the 'Media'.

It is a really quite graphic depiction of modern realities and ought to be giving pause to all those political scientists and academic lecturers who continue to assume and assert that the mere fact of the existence of the ballot box and bi-decadal mass voting exercises somehow constitutes a realistic system of democracy.

It is a new form of power, especially commercial (which was only introduced in 1955), as distinct from public service television, and far from being accountable to the people is largely determining their tastes, standards and values. To quote Sampson, 'People's television had created television's people.'

The assumed right of mass journals, radio and TV to promote values and propensities on a mass scale with no regard for the public weal, in the name of free speech, has had a long and disastrous innings. There is no need to question the right of private individuals to be free to publish and broadcast their views on any subject they may choose; what concerns us here is when that undisputed individual right is assumed to be the unquestioned prerogative of giant commercial bodies or mass political organisations. The mass media, unlike the individual voice, wields enormous power; it is power being used to project a barrage of tendentiousness on to a mass and largely defenceless audience. It is based on the principle that the inviolable rights of an individual can be assumed by any immensely powerful organisation, which can then use those 'rights' to trample at will on the social structure; as a result the printing press, broadcasting and T.V. are forms of power which are determining the very nature of society itself. How is that power used?

Democracy is assumed to be government *by* the people! And it is pertinent to ask in what way are the people governing this relatively new and imposing form of power? The current cant has it that people control it by market pressures; they buy the mass newspaper or tune in to the radio or TV channel of their choice. What could be more democratic?

It is a question which ignores the very nature of the power being wielded and the objectives for which it is being used. Democracy presupposes everyone has an equal voice. On a centralised mass scale it is impossible to realise such equality and especially so in relation to the media. The artefacts of media projection generally involve the investment of large sums of money; in June 2004 for example the UK Telegraph Newspaper Group was purchased for £7,665 million.

Only a tiny minority can have access to such sums and since ordinarily the purpose of investment is to make as much profit as possible, it is reasonable to suppose that the policies of the media outlets will tend to focus on matters which will enhance that objective.

The Media and Motoring

Two questions arise here; how can the media avoid using its immense power to cultivate and project the values which sustain its overall quest? How can it avoid conditioning the public consciousness to accept the *mores* of profit-seeking as a supreme social objective?

Life in modern so called developed societies is dominated by the continuous and highly skilled propaganda of advertising in its promotion of an exaggerated emphasis on the acquisition of material goods, and the use of such services as travel, as an ultimate purpose of living. It does this regardless of the social consequences or indeed of any other consequences except its own enrichment. So the non-stop promotion of car ownership will ignore the effects on global warming, its effects on distorting and often destroying social relationships and community structures, on family life, on the deliberate run-down of finite resources such as oil and the consequent impoverishment of future generations, on the high rate of accidents;[2] on the distortion of priorities in relation to public rail services, the extension of the working day by car commuting, with its concomitant of stress of mind and body and, not least, the perpetual ordeal of noise, stink and poisoned air suffered by millions who live alongside busy urban roads.

We have the media to thank for the widespread acceptance of the car as a sign of progress and that it gives millions the illusion of freedom, if only to queue for hours on increasingly crowded motorways. It is the media which dazzles the gullible with full page pictures of the latest models, with its 'motoring' supplements, its endless emphasis on the need for more and better motorways, its continuous chatter about this or that problem of motoring facilities as though human life would be impossible without them. It ignores that the vast majority of the human race does not own a car and is unlikely ever to do so, if only because in a matter of a decade or so oil prices, governed by increasing demand against declining reserves, are likely to put fuel beyond the reach of many of even the starry-eyed

[2]   In the UK alone there are 3,500 car accident fatalities a year and of course many more cases of serious injury often involving being crippled for life.

millions who regard unlimited consumption of this finite resource in a finite world as an inalienable part of their birthright. Indeed the car era is likely to prove only too transient; what erupts suddenly in history is apt to disappear at much the same rate.

But how has the widespread acceptance of this essentially socially and environmentally destructive artefact been achieved? When, at every point of the compass, the citizen is bombarded with highly tendentious 'information' that assumes the car is a perfectly normal and acceptable means of transport, how is the citizen dependent on such sources for his news of public events, to judge otherwise? When has there ever been a prolonged, far-reaching public debate in the media to convey the moral options and to enable the citizen to make an informed judgement? The fact is the media is not concerned with informed judgement, only with the promotion of commercial interest. It is not interested in the social interest, only in a quest for more money, and that quest simply buries the public good not only in matters of transport, but in food, health and the general consumerist lifestyle which currently, albeit temporarily, enslaves millions.

Let us be clear that the rights of freedom of expression are vital to the individual. He needs them to achieve whatever measure of fulfilment is within his reach, his intent in using any such right is that he may live more fully and assert his humanity. The intent of any commercial organisation in assuming its entitlement to operate within the framework of any such rights is simply to make money, and the general tendency in this case is to do so by constantly expanding the number of readers, viewers or listeners exposed to its message and to limit their freedom of choice by all the highly skilled artifices of mass persuasion they can deploy.

Since much of the money and of course much of the profit is derived from advertising, and the charges for advertisements are strictly related to the numbers of those exposed to them, it results in the strenuous attempts constantly made to increase those numbers. But at what cost to society, its values, its health and its future? We are back to the consideration that the battle, for it is a battle, to increase numbers involves a constant pandering to the tastes, aptitudes, values and dispositions of the lowest common denominator of the mass taste rather than to the highest common factor of discernment and judgement and ultimately of course, rather than enhancing the rights of free expression it is using such rights in ways which must eventually destroy them. Why? Because the definition of 'rights', their observation and promotion, is one of the great attributes of civilisation; it depends on civilised values, on respect for others, on integrity of utterance and behaviour. It is in short a fundamental aspect of morality and any civilisation with no respect for morality is a dying one.

Hence the presumption of commercial bodies to act as they will within the framework of morally inspired rights of individual expression can only lead to the destruction of any sense of moral choice, for what ensues, what all too clearly has ensued, is a competitive orgy of mass debasement and general disassociation of moral standards in relation to the workings of the social order, standards it has taken centuries to establish.

Competition

The voice of the market may be said to have its due place in a free society; but we have yet to reach a stage of moral grandeur where each member gives freely of his services in the confident expectation that he will be assured of the necessities, comforts and services he requires in return. There will always be those readier to exploit market opportunities than to serve society in other ways, and more than two centuries ago Adam Smith sought to justify such activity on the grounds that if each trader sought to maximise his advantage the element of competitive pricing would itself help to keep any propensity to seek undue profit in check. He was well aware of the moral status of entrepreneurship but was sublimely confident that the market itself via competition would solve the problem.

But it hasn't and it doesn't. He assumed that the market would be in a constant state of lively equilibrium, and in doing so overlooked that in any competitive market struggle those with a sharper eye for market realities and possibilities would always be ready to take advantage of those traders who might lack such abilities. In short, he overlooked that in a competitive market there were important forces at work besides that of price regulation and that in consequence there would be winners, and of course losers, and that one consequence of winning was to make the winner bigger and, as the loser went to the wall, to become a more powerful market force. And even this has proved to be not the end of the process, it has become indeed generally but a beginning; for the winner will then find himself competing with other winners from which will emerge an even bigger winner who will then be competing with other bigger winners, by a process of mergers, takeovers and other forms of elimination.

Ultimately, the biggest winners will come to dominate the market in semi-monopolistic, or even outright monopoly conditions.

This is not theory or speculation, but modern history, and in the early years of a new millennium we are confronted with such forces of monopolistic control in all the dominant sectors of the economy, and not least, in the field of mass media operation. What Smith also overlooked was the factor of scale. He was unable to see that whilst his argument about the self-regulating role of competition (the 'invisible hand') in market activity in a localised community was perfectly valid, provided the market remained local and competitive on a small scale, it would become absurd when the scale of the market expanded to embrace the activities of giant nations or enterprises on a global scale.

Political Monopoly

A similar process is clearly at work in politics; in an electorate of many millions there is scope for as many opinions about any of the matters of public policy. In *mass* conditions members of Parliament are not elected for their representative capacities in relation to these opinions, desirable as that might be; they are elected as political party representatives and in the nature of things in mass conditions there will not be hundreds or thousands, or indeed hundreds of thousands of parties. The smaller ones will either be subsumed into anonymity in one mass party or another, or sidelined into ineffectuality altogether. The winners will win their way to a semi-monopolistic status where the essential differences of the policies they avow become increasingly hard to detect. In the UK today there are three main mass parties and it is bemusing to note that none of them shows any serious sign of concern or commitment to confront any of the five crisis factors indicated at the beginning of this work.

It is also an indicator of the essential powerlessness of the individual citizen that all three are supporters, either with active campaigning or, as with the older Conservative party, by passivity and silence, of the commercially and market-inspired plot (there really is no other adequate word to indicate its nature) to destroy what remnants of democratic control residually remain in the different nation states of Europe, by merging them into a single entity based on the capital of Belgium.

It is beside the point that successive opinion polls have indicated a marked majority hostility to what is afoot, nor that the UK referendum in 1975 on joining the common market secured only a marginal assenting vote, itself based on repeated assurances that Britain was simply joining a 'market', that no surrender of sovereignty was involved at all, and that the referendum 'campaign' was backed by a massive promotional propaganda drive, using for the most part the taxpayers own money. It is also not without relevance that even the constitution of a local bowls club will ordinarily contain a provision that it might require a two thirds majority to secure any proposed alteration to its rules.

We are here not in the realm of values, morals, rights, opinions or any other attribute of democratic order; we are in the realm of power and that power is largely in the hands of the big winners, both economic and political. It is not, nor in centralised mass terms, can it ever be, in the hands of the individual citizen.

Media Priorities

If this is one of the major problems confronting the modern world it is also one hardly, if ever, discussed in mass media outlets; why, after all, should they be expected to question the very assumptions on which the success of their work rests? It is the kind of silence which infects our political and economic processes at many levels simply because it suppresses consideration of what those processes *are*, as distinct from what they do.

No answer to it can fail to involve proposals that enable democracy to function. The exercise of any 'right' does not thereby justify an acceptance of its abuse, and we have to ask how the immense power implicit in media operations can be made subject to local community influence and control. In posing the question we have to note that most media outlets are only secondarily agents of what they purport to be. Newspapers do not just purvey news; they convey a great deal more comment and discussion. Since the viability of the exercise is dependent on the readiness of advertisers to pay to advertise, it follows that the process of selection of news and comment will be of a nature that does not adversely affect the interests of the advertisers. Why give undue prominence to global warming, for example, when it is caused by industrial emissions of which mass motoring and mass aeroplane journeys are a significant contributory factor, when it may lead to a decline in lucrative advertisements for cars or air travel?

The range of selection, to say nothing of comment, is obviously enormous. What items shall be stressed and perhaps given banner headlines? What shall be relegated to a minor sub-paragraph, or not mentioned at all? On this basis it is evident that an utterly distorted picture of events is being projected, which leads in turn to a mass acceptation of that distortion. Peoples' judgements are consequently based not so much on facts, as on perceived facts; and the media functions to hone that perception to its own concerns and values. How else to account for the absence of any effective mass movements against motoring, or against a consumerist lifestyle in terms of dress, food or home furnishing, which is destroying the possibility of a decent life for anyone? Or against the whole works of the Europlot, the aim of which is to destroy such degrees of democracy as continue to exist in separate European countries by subsuming their power of sovereignty and independence into the power of a new European superstate, one gestated by money-power to serve the concerns of money-power? Or against the ongoing preparation for another global war, now that nearly thirty nations have a nuclear capability and bombs, tanks, guns and battleships are being produced in ever greater numbers?

Responsibility

There is an inference here from prevailing media practice that people don't really much mind about the high roads on which we are travelling to mass starvation on a global scale because of our chemicalised and industrialised abuse of the only environment we have, or that their children will be exposed to measureless degrees of impoverishment and hardship because of the way we are squandering the finite resources of what is, after all, a finite world. Nor do they have any qualms or concern about the inevitable prospect of being incinerated in their homes as towns and cities are destroyed by modern war weaponry. They are far more interested in all the gory details of the exploits of a serial murderer, or the love affairs of a well known entertainer, or the sex life of a prominent politician, or the fate of one football team or another. It may well be averred that indeed most of them are, and if that is true, what degree of responsibility do our media moguls have in failing to alert them to the nature of the doomsday scenario that has today become the backdrop of all our lives?

It is not that ordinary media people don't care, even if it is true many of them don't care. The fact is that they cannot afford to care, they are caught in an ongoing trap of institutionalised power imperatives that ordain the content of their work. It is now urgent that we cut back factory production and the mass marketing and use of its products if civilisation is to survive. But that is a long-term prospect to which media people, like so many others, can do no proper justice if the effects on 'growth', jobs, incomes, public services and other attributes of a materially affluent lifestyle are not to be diminished.

In all this we are apt to overlook that industry has sprung from a world of small, local workshops, of small farms, of production by hand tools and by labour-intensive processes. The need to revert to these beginnings if the environment is to survive the punishment now being inflicted on it will only be resisted by those who know nothing about the problem. But they include masses of people who will 'lose their jobs'; albeit they will be freed for other jobs yielding a greater sense of well-being. More importantly newspapers will perhaps lose readers and TV channels will lose viewers, and not least politicians will lose votes. All of them are on a ratchet of self-destruction they have themselves created and from which they cannot escape without ceasing to achieve the kinds of success they now dedicate the mainspring of their lives to pursuing.

An Alternative

Within the current framework of values it is possible that very little can be changed that will significantly change the general trend. Can we then create another framework? We have to recognise the human personality is a compound of propensities which may be said to stretch across the entire gamut of options, and that the advance of civilisation is a constant struggle to rise above the brute, the coarse and even the merely passive in us all, and to reach out for what can refine and ennoble. All through history it has always been a struggle which has been led by a minority; an isolated genius in any field may show the way, a responsive minority may seek to follow and gradually a transformation of the whole may be affected.

We may note that just as Bach's music has had the profoundest effects on musical experience even in the field of pop, whose adherents may never have heard of him, so Shakespeare's language has influenced the development of everyday speech for masses of people who might even repudiate any concern for his works. The essential point to note is that quality is generally the concern of a minority and that changes of outlook which lead to any improvement are generally affected in the majority by a largely unreflecting and even unconscious process, it is a process which calls into question the role of leadership in effecting any change at all.

On a mass basis, and we must never cease to stress the importance of the qualification, such moves for change are generally essayed by commercially or politically interested parties with an eye to the main chance. Moral leadership is another matter altogether and by an inverse process, despite all the claptrap about mass democracy, masses of ordinary people are more divorced from it than they have ever been. Indeed how could it be otherwise when all the main means of communication are in the grip of largely amoral forces whilst people are increasingly isolated from each other and thus out of reach of the still small voice that might evoke the leadership they so evidently lack?

Such leadership today is largely that of the dissenting voice of the articulate and alert-minded citizen, all too often dismissed (by the media moguls and their hacks) as cranks, misfits, romantics, agitators, rebels or even, in the parlance of 21st Century vernacular, terrorists.

In former times great causes might be articulated by small groups of inspired, dedicated and disinterested reformers; it is their work which has seen slavery abolished, at least in formal terms, and seen reform in many other spheres such as prisons, hospitals, schools, work, law, the status of womankind, and so on. Even though they might work against the stream of current perceptions many of their aims have come to prevail, but it took time, in some cases generations.

Today we are in a race against time to abandon the drive that sustains the entire complex of an industrialised civilisation, as well as the assumptions, such as they are, on which it is based before its own excesses proceed to prompt its disintegration.

The media has largely supplanted, where it has not destroyed, the role of the church, the family and the community, in establishing the prevailing moral principles which people live, and has set standards of behaviour and judgement far more pervasively and effectively than any Caesar, Stalin or Hitler was ever able to achieve. Yet, as we have seen, it is part of the cruel idiocy of our times that this power is very largely in the hands of people who desire to use it for no other purpose than to make money, an objective they are unable to pursue without debasing whatever standards society may have achieved.

Clearly it is a problem demanding a swift, wide-ranging transformation, but what in practice can be done? How, for example, do we tackle the problem of the abuse of power implicit in the very existence of mass circulation newspapers? How do we accomplish any sort of responsible control that does not throw the baby of freedom out with the bathwater of social reform? As in all other matters where changes are in sight which will remedy the abuse of power, care must be taken to avoid projecting solutions on a national or international scale which ignore the law of unintended effects, and which have the effect of replicating the conditions which have fostered the abuse to begin with. We need to be clear that our concern is to enable local communities to exercise their own judgement to control by human-scale division to one degree or other the huge forces now dominating all our lives, and over which they currently have little or no control at all.

It would be easy to specify legislation to restrict the ownership of any mass circulation publication by insisting no person or company may own more than one such publication at any time; or that publications having a circulation of more than a given number must admit locally elected representation and representatives of the workforce to voting rights on the board of management. Whatever the merits or practicalities of such proposals they breathe an air of top-down restrictionism suggesting its own need to seek alternatives.

Local Differences

On this, if local communities are to to empower ed, one cannot afford to overlook that since communities will have different views, they will inevitably project different solutions; if only for this reason they need to be at liberty to take whatever measures seem to them appropriate. Will some favour a selective tax on commercial advertising? And if so how will the interests of educational and cultural concerns be safeguarded? Or will they favour a progressive circulation tax which rises disproportionately with increases in sales?

Will some feel a need to subsidise heavily their own local journals, linked perhaps with training centres for local, community-conscious journalists? Or provide a free community-funded news service? Perhaps; but newspapers have long since ceased to regard the dissemination of news as their primary role; today that role is predominantly one of entertainment, and specially with the tabloids, of titillation. If the problems here of securing some degree of social control on the basis of respect for freedom are considerable, it does not mean they should be shirked, nor that we should fail to maintain a distinction between the sacrosanct rights of the individual and the legal rights of limited liability companies to use those rights to secure advantages for their shareholders.

The distinction becomes even more important when considering the problems of a decent social input into radio and television. Today it is impossible for any local community to protect itself from receiving material which may damage its interests or the standards it may set itself, and it will be noted that even to point to such consideration leads to the quicksand of discussion on what constitutes freedom.

Today it is technically possible for any agency to establish itself anywhere to transmit programmes about anything to any other part of the world. No community can avoid being targeted via satellite or other means from anywhere else with anything, and this is already evident from the computerised use of websites and emails.

What is really happening here is technology out of control and in some major respects, technology simply in a frenzy of madness. Society, any society, is first and foremost a moral entity; it lives and can only live, on the basis of certain moral principles, themselves a feature of every society that has ever existed. Of course there have been times when those principles have been mocked, scorned, abused or even denied, but in every case events have exacted their own price and it is society itself which has subsequently sought to restore a moral momentum to its workings.

It was able to do this because the voice of conscience could sooner or later make itself heard and because there was a capacity within the structure of society which enabled a response to be made. The process in historical terms might be one of fits and starts, of lapses into conditions of barbarism, but always the momentum was there, however repressed, however bleak and cruel the terror that might prevail, so that today there are vast libraries of social literature which witness to human striving for the supremacy of moral law, just as there is a vast body of legal enactments which seeks to underpin that same thrust.

Some measure of the extent of the changes in outlook in the modern era can be seen from Napoleon's views in 1798, that 'In war, moral considerations make up three-quarters of the game: the relative balance of manpower accounts only for the remaining quarter.' Would Churchill, Hitler, Stalin or Roosevelt have subscribed to that view in 1940? What governed the decisions of any of them? Morality — or power?

Over two hundred years ago Kant could declare, 'Two things fill the mind with ever increasing awe and wonder; the starry heavens above me and the moral law within me', an observation which would be dismissed today by media magnates as being irrelevant to what fills their minds and their products as they quest for ever higher ratings or readerships.

Morality and The Microchip

If technical facility makes serious localised control of media standards all but impossible, so that such standards as any local community may wish to uphold are under continuous assault from exterior commercial forces, are they then powerless to resist?

Before answering the question it is important to note the extent to which technical advance in the fields of computers and communication have enormously increased the powers of centralised governmental surveillance. It is not commonly known that every single telephone conversation, even by mobile phones, can be recorded, is indeed generally recorded, and in some cases is required by law to be recorded. The same facility is exercised with computers, not only in emails and on websites, but to a different degree, with the computers themselves, since even when matter on a screen is 'deleted' it remains in the `memory' of the machine. Also relevant to this is the ever increasing use of cameras and other surveillance devices, especially in public places; indeed it is probable that today no citizen in going about his ordinary business in any urban centre is ever free from such focus, and the standard plea is always that it helps to check law-breaking.

Perhaps its does, and if it does we cannot overlook or ignore the cost of doing so, for such means are creating a vast new power of surveillance over every aspect of a citizen's life, and in the hands of centralised authorities on a scale which puts them beyond the reach of effective democratic citizen control. Nor should we ignore the extent to which such means have failed to achieve the objectives for which they have been employed.

A thug government is one which exercises power with no regard for moral constraint. Such governments have been one of the horrific aspects of much of twentieth century life, as any Russian, German, Chinese or East European citizen would have been only too ready to acknowledge, and the same sort of government is still very much with us today. It is ordinary political realism to acknowledge that the governments of all giant states, including the leading members of the 'European' exercise based in Brussels and that of the USA, China, Russia and India, to name only some of the largest, do not differ in kind from the monstrous regimes of Hitler and Stalin, only in degree. Given the prevailing global trends to excess in almost every sphere that government can reach it would be sanguine to suppose that the days of such government are likely soon to be numbered.

The reverse is only too probable: as popular discontent erupts, as different forms of excess create an inevitable breakdown in monetary systems, in food, water and oil supplies, and as mass unemployment and destitution multiply, we have to see those nominally in control at the centre will have ample cause to feel beleaguered. Inevitably, reform movements will arise and seek to challenge those in command and to change things. In the past however, governments used spies, *agents provocateurs*, informers and an established network of intelligence-gathering to defend their power; how much of this will now be necessary? We must suppose that every dissident, every person who has ever uttered a word of criticism of the established powers, will already be known to them. A mere pressing of a finger on a keyboard will codify and identify them.

It has been seen with sickening clarity what thug government is capable of doing with the power of technology and mass information in its hands. How in Hitler's Germany bureaucrats, scientists, architects, transport officials and military power could be used to build and operate camps in which millions of fellow human beings, men, women, adolescents, children and babes in arms, were deliberately done to death. Of what will such governments be capable when in control of the information now available via computers?

It is possible that new technical developments may enable citizen groups to develop forms of resistance to this new and pervasive power and so redress the balance in favour of the small and the local against the big and the centralised. We would be wise not to bet on it. Rather is it necessary to develop and extend the decision-making power at the local level as a matter of the utmost urgency. Gandhi's oft-quoted observation 'You cannot have morality without community' takes on today its own note of imperative realism. Morality is, after all, a force, perhaps one of the strongest in the historic record, but since it can only operate effectively within a community structure where personal relationships predominate over all other factors within human control, the case for making community power our greatest political concern may be said to take precedence over all other considerations if our civilisation is to survive and advance.

This is not a matter requiring our attention after we have surrendered our time and our energies to all the other claims on our lives;

we need to give it the maximum focus now, now, now, if only because it is the brightest hope we have in a rapidly darkening sky. Somehow or other the individual citizen must find his voice amid the prevailing cacophony and make it heard. He must come to see that confronted with highly centralised forces on a mass scale he will always be powerless to direct or control them, however many times he exercises his right to vote. He must see that citizen control can only be adequately exercised when the scale of things matches his humanity; once it exceed those limits he is in the grip of the controlling forces at the centre. Modern history is eloquent that those forces will pursue immediate objectives of money and power regardless of any moral considerations, of any considerations relating to citizen interest or to the long term interests of society as a whole. The keynote of these forces is that of excess, whether in terms of a propensity for war, for environmental despoliation, for resource wastage, or social dislocation and abuse. That tendency to excess is here a function of the scale on which these forces operate, it is the scale which must be reduced if man will exercise the control he needs to achieve the glittering prizes of social grandeur he has always sought.

Media Democracy

This discussion has sought to emphasise the extent to which a money-making media is helping to reinforce centralised government powers by refusing to question the basic assumptions on which those powers are exercised and by maintaining an emphatic silence on any serious discussion which might project any assumptions involving the exercise of citizen power, especially if it might conflict with media regard for immediate monetary prospects.

How can such citizen power be made to operate? In general terms there is a need to insist on a recognition that the role of the media is not simply one of transmitting information, it is also a powerful instrument for educating, and for promoting the values that can advance civilisation. In this light there is a clear need to put its workings largely in the hands of societies' teachers, artists, philosophers, writers, thinkers and those with a concern for the moral and ethical standards of society at large.

How will their work be funded? It will be funded by the citizenry either through taxation or licence fees from the general level of money in circulation or from sales, as already is the case. But it needs to be noted that the present operations involve an enormous expenditure not only of money, but of professionalized advertising skills exercised for very high fees, to say nothing of paper and other resources, and most of which is either unnecessary or undesirable or both.

A media devoted to public excellence rather than to private profit will be able to create an entirely new dynamic and cultural emphasis in public life But change can only be effected for the better when there is a clear perception of the goals aimed for. One may note in passing the enormous price paid in terms of human suffering and human life when socialists, communists, and revolutionaries of many kinds have sought to employ the machinery of the state to achieve their goals in the absence of any such clarity of objectives.

The promotion of the decision-making power of people in their local communities must be a primary goal of any serious concern to improve the human lot, even if that power is used in ways which may sometimes be unacceptable in terms of decent standards. Tyranny for example can be a feature of local government even if not so pervasive and all-embracing as it tends to be on a national level.

But in such regard there is an important difference. Most people for most of the time tend to be passive and acquiescent under any form of government. In national terms governments are prone to exploit this passivity for whatever purposes they seek, however unworthy they may be, and the minority who may object and seek improvement can easily be ignored if not silenced. In empowered local terms 'Papworth's Law' is at work: 'The smaller the unit the larger the significance of the individual member'. Smallness itself helps to empower the individual and it is not difficult to see how a crusading minority in a local community can make its voice heard and make an effective impact in ways which on a giant mass scale are far more difficult to achieve, where indeed they are possible at all.

It is necessary also to take account of the extent to which local talents and abilities are so effectively stifled and negated under national arrangements and which, when local power is operative, would be employed to the full. If a local community of two or three thousand were charged with responsibility for running its own schools and empowered with local funding decisions, why should it be supposed there would be any lack of concern among its members to ensure the highest possible standards and that the policies pursued would reflect local needs rather than bureaucratically determined national targets? What could be expected to emerge from local power is a concern for excellence which would be able to find expression and revitalise local affairs in ways no national power could begin to rival.

What we have been discussing here bristles with urgent questions at every point. It betokens the need for a continuous wide-ranging and exhaustive debate, one that should be engaging the involvement of numerous concerned people whose energies are currently being frittered away on such things, for example, as 'peace' campaigns. There have been peace organisations, peace movements, peace publications and peace demonstrations, to say nothing of peace marches, meetings, conferences, protests, petitions and the like for well over two generations. When will it dawn on these ardent activists that in human affairs the shortest distance between two points is seldom a straight line, that knee-jerk reactions to whatever war policies a government may be pursuing is one thing, even as they continue to ignore that after generations of such dedicated activity the danger of bigger and more disastrous wars is now greater than it has ever been.

Or those who campaign for 'fair trade' or, believe it or not, to 'Make Poverty History'. When will they grasp they can make only a marginal impact on the problems they are so energetically seeking to solve or the cause they seek to espouse, not least when we are already in the opening stages of a cataclysm of poverty that will engulf the lives of billions in further degrees of want to an extent which there is no human precedent? When will they and others dedicated to an entire gamut of 'good causes' however justified their concern, however dedicated their efforts and however altruistic their motives, grasp that such concern is largely irrelevant and that they are confronting a whirlwind of social disintegration because the power to determine the direction of our social order is in the hands of blinkered social misfits, morally obtuse dwarfs and criminally motivated morons who have eyes, ears and noses for nothing but the aggrandisement of their appetites for profit or power or both?

When will they grasp that the legitimacy of their concerns can only find effective expression in resolving the problem of power, social, economic and political power, so that it is in safe hands subject to decent citizen moral judgement and one that can only be effected when the citizen can operate the levers of power, however miniscule, in his or her own local community?

And if there is this desperate need for such reformers to get their act together, what are we to say to all those dedicated acolytes of the academic world, today more numerous than they have ever been, or all those full time, fully paid ministers of religion of one God or one belief system or ritual or another, who steadfastly toil away at their career concerns as though they can assume they live in a safe house when the entire structure is disintegrating under their noses?

Where is the quest for wisdom of the academics? There are more of them than at any previous time in history! Where are the books, papers, publications, conferences and debates on what is happening and where we are going? Why do they not all bestir themselves and raise questions about the fundamentally debased intellectual and moral orientation of this tragic drift of our social order to an inevitable hell-on-earth if we do not change our ways and change the thinking on which those ways are based before we are totally undone?

Perhaps the Christian clergy have a special concern here. They, after all, promote a prophet who abjured us all, if we may resort to his own words:

> *Thou shalt love the Lord thy God with all thy heart, and with all thy soul, and with all thy mind: This is the first and great commandment. And the second is like unto it, Thou shalt love thy neighbour as thyself. On these two commandments hang all the law and the prophets.*[3]

That is surely simple enough, love God and love your neighbour. With the best will in the world not easy abjurations to follow. I can think of several 'neighbours' with whom I would not want to share my supper table, but where is the clerical voice, the clerical concern, or the clerical involvement when the entire structure and impetus of our organised lives is perpetrating the destruction of God's creation? How else can we 'love God' except by straining every nerve to protect and revere the creation He has bequeathed us? And how can we 'love our neighbour' when dominant political and economic forces are perpetrating the destruction of neighbour relationships and neighbourly community structures? How can you 'love your neighbour' if he or she does not exist as we increasingly live as strangers to each other?

There are five Archbishops and sixty seven Bishops of the Church of England in Britain alone, never mind about the Catholic Church and the non-conformists. Never mind each Bishop appears to have a support staff, often involving Area Bishops, Suffragan Bishops, Assistant Bishops, Deans, Vice Deans, Archdeacons, Diocesan Secretaries and other functionaries. What are they doing in a social

---

[3]   Matthew 22:37–40

order which is repudiating the very basis of the faith they are supposed to be promoting? They are all adequately salaried, some live in palaces even, but where is their voice? Their concern? Their involvement? Or for that matter that of their thousands of beneficed clergy? Their silence is truly deafening and can only prompt one to wonder.

Here is a body established for no other purpose than to promote the teachings of its founder. Its voice is equipped with a vast endowment of some of the most glorious architecture, music and moral wisdom the world has ever seen, equipped with authority and tradition, and with money enough to maintain a huge army of paid acolytes and assistants, confronted with forces actively promoting social institutions and policies having the effect of repudiating every one of its founder's teachings, a repudiation which is breeding every symptom of moral suffering and decay as the society to which it professes to give moral leadership is clearly staggering blindly to ultimate degrees of total disintegration and collapse.

Its voice appears to be heard with all the dynamic, clarion-call, resonances of a dying tadpole. What on earth do all these otherwise functionless devotees who appear never to miss a dinner think they are doing? Where do they think they are going when their collective voice has all the dynamic urgency of a comatose caterpillar?

To do them justice they are quite unaware that the sum total of their profession has the effect of amounting to little more than a gigantic confidence trick; they have no more recognition of the realities of their role, or of the aid they are giving to the hordes of Satan, than a trapped fly in glue. They are just not aware that they are unaware, and in consequence display no vestige of concern, commitment or even curiosity to express the slightest readiness to respond.

To do them further justice they appear to be equally unaware that when the Church is closely identified in the popular mind with the powers of the secular authority of the state, it cannot fail to share in a general loss of prestige and respect when that authority ceases to be an effective guardian of the general public interest and proceeds to govern in terms devoid of any decent moral principle.

Chapter Eight

The Democratic Deficit

The role of money. – Investment decisions and circular reasoning. – Usury important role. – Other new forms of power. – Central government power. – Illusion of democracy. – The EUroplot – Democracy a basic social necessity.

Democratic Credit Control

No work seeking to clarify problems of power in society which fails to take account of the role of money can expect to be taken with any seriousness. The importance of money does not stem from its intrinsic value, or from the notional value any particular unit of it may express. Its real power stems not from its use as a medium of exchange, for besides gold, silver, notes or coinage, the variety of items which has been used to serve this function is practically beyond reckoning. Most of them, whether shells, beads, salt or whatever, possessed the degree of scarcity which bestowed a particular value on them, and they served the needs of particular societies without raising problems involving the democratic deployment of the power to control their supply to undue prominence.

Modern money facilities, originally based on precious metals and banknotes, are different, and raise problems of power of control to enormous heights because that they can be used to make loans and to 'earn' interest. These facilities make modern banking systems possible and enable banks to establish a powerful controlling position in the economic life of any community. They are enabled to do so by their power to grant or withhold credit, to make or withhold loans on which the borrower, in addition to repaying the loan must also pay a rate of interest determined by the lender.

The history of the progression of banking practice has been from lending actual sums of gold and silver, to lending bank notes promising to pay a given sum of such metals, notes issued on the basis of actual reserves of precious metals in its vaults, and thence to the modern practice of issuing loans backed by no precious metals at all but simply on the authority of the institution making the loan, itself nominally backed by the deposits made by other customers.

What is noteworthy is the extent to which modern societies have become dependent for their everyday workings on a highly central-ised system of the power to make loans by simply entering figures indicating the size of the loan in the bank's records. It is a process which would seem capable of apparently infinite immediate expan-sion, if the limits of what is after all a finite world are ignored. The catch of course is that if the process of lending is pursued far enough a society will find itself awash with credit, which in turn will raise problems about the value of the currency itself as inflation takes off and threatens to destroy it.

It is not only enterprising individuals who borrow money with which to spend or speculate, governments are in the same game. The US federal debt in 2005 totals a staggering $7 trillion, and the British government's debt now amounts to £437.4 billion. In Britain house prices are currently soaring, largely because banks are ready to lend people money to buy provided they pay a due rate of interest, cur-rently codified as a mortgage. The Banks decide who shall own a house, but they decide a great many other things too, such as in which directions investment based on borrowed money, ('credit'), shall take. Shall it be for decent home-grown food produced by small local farmers? Or for giant firms bestriding the world like a colossus to promote prairie-type agricultural production in remote countries with the liberal application of chemicals, where the lower unit costs achieved by this abuse of the soil enables the produce to be flown in to undercut local farmers' prices and drive them to bankruptcy?

Shall investment be for more roads or for better railways? For giant clothing factories in Asia manned by underpaid, overworked and non-unionised labour, often children, or for local workshops? For guns and bombs or for schools and libraries? A selective pursuit of quality or a mindless scramble for quantity? Simply to raise such questions is a reminder that economics is a function determining the use of resources rather than a bogus science seeking to grapple with statistics about money. What else can the distinction between the two approaches be but one of adopting a policy of moral commit-ment, or one of moral abandonment.

Resource Utilisation Objectives

Money economics is based on a process of circular reasoning involv-ing a totally unreal assumption that the supply of resources is of infinite capacity. All that matters is whether a given investment of a given sum of money will produce more money to enable more investment to be made to produce more money, and so on. It is a process of reasoning utterly divorced from any consideration about the wise use of resources, the quality of peoples lives or the general nature and condition of the social order, to say nothing of the extent to which it facilitates abuse of the environment.

Any consideration of what may be the wisest use of resources is of course posing the question of what they are being used *for*? Is the proposed use likely to benefit society at large, or merely enrich a well-placed minority? Does it take account of any disruption of the social order and of community life? Or the extent the undue rush to consume an available resource may result in the impoverishment of future generations?

We are at once confronted not with the impersonal abstractions of monetary calculations, but with the greatest unsolved (and probably insoluble) problem that has beset us through the ages, of seeking to conduct economic activity on a mass basis in terms of a moral code. What shall that code be? Men have grappled with the problem down the centuries and we are as far from resolving it in the twenty first century as we were in the first.

Usury

But at least in former times the sages and saints of different periods did try, and what should engage our attention today is the degree to which their scholarship and their moral judgements focused on the use and abuse of monetary credit or, as they termed it, usury. Their judgement was that it was immoral and should be forbidden. It seemed to them quite wrong that by lending money to someone in need the lender should be able to reap the fruits of the labour of the borrower by charging interest on the loan. So in Jewish and Muslim scriptures usury is declared immoral and such judgement was the basis of many legal enactments which outlawed the practice.

The Christian response was also to condemn it in practice, although the only references to it in the gospel accounts are two which inscrutably relate the same story with the same moral, to the effect that a servant who refrained from using money entrusted to him by his master and who failed to increase it by taking it to a usurer, was condemned 'as wicked and slothful' and 'cast into outer darkness'. [1]

Whatever the intended moral of this curious account there can be no doubt that Christian teaching over the centuries was emphatically opposed to the practice of usury, which was roundly condemned as 'covetousness' and as being one of the seven deadly sins. And its condemnation was forcibly expressed in a series of legal enactments, both secular and ecclesiastical, which were operative until the closing years of the reign of the first Queen Elizabeth.

The prohibitions were in any case only partial and were mainly designed to protect the small unfortunates against the grasp of the extortioners; but big banking houses across Europe did not cease to do big business by accommodating the needs of big rulers and potentates. Nevertheless the late Elizabethan laws, which effectively ended the prohibition, were already long under assault from the powerful surge of the needs of both borrowers and lenders seeking to take advantage of the expanding trade which an influx of gold from the New World and the technical improvements in navigation had done so much to stimulate.

The fact remains that this repeal constitutes an imposing watershed in the history of the modern world. For at least fifteen centuries, churchmen and church-inspired secular authorities had sought to control the forces embodied in the practice of usury, and we need to ask, 'Why?'

For answer we have to match their fears and apprehensions against the full nature of the global crisis with which we are battling today. They were concerned with the preservation of a social structure based on a frank acknowledgement of class division: peasants had their role and place, as did craftsmen and merchants, and as did a feudal aristocracy. The higher should not oppress the lower and usury was objectionable because it was used to do just that.

Even more, usury, if allowed to flourish, might enable money and money concerns to set at naught the cardinal moral teachings of the Church, might indeed, come to dominate the entire workings of the social order at the expense of its moral foundations. This assertion is partly speculative, but how otherwise to account for the frenzy of denunciation to which usury was subjected down the centuries? It was as if there was an awareness that here was a force which reached far beyond the contract for debt and repayment between two indi-

---

[1]   Matthew 25:14 and also Luke 19:12

viduals, one which might herald a society dominated by money and money interests rather than by the moral teachings of the Church.

Those teachings may have promoted the class distinctions of the time which are no longer acceptable, and they may have often been betrayed in practice by Church authorities themselves. The operations of the Spanish Inquisition, with all the grisly accompaniments of torture and expropriation of wealthy landowners on the basis of trumped up charges of heresy, for example was little more than a land racket, but the Church's teaching of love of neighbour was alive, as was its own assurance that life had meaning and that the workings of society needed to express it.

Money Control and Democracy

The crucial question however, that needed to be raised and wasn't, was not whether usury should be permitted or outlawed, since the rising class of speculators and banks ensured it would prevail anyway, but how it should be controlled; controlled for purposes that enriched society rather than undermined it.

On this, the Church fell silent. In Tawney's crisp aphorism, 'The Church said nothing because it had nothing to say'. Today, centuries later, we are reaping the bitter fruits of that silence, for usury has proved to be the steel scaffolding of a wholly new structure of society, one built on the foundations of centuries of resplendent moral and cultural endeavour, and which in turn has proceeded to reduce them to a virtual nullity. The monster of usury, freed from its former shackles, has confirmed the worst fears of the sages and divines of old who foresaw that once legitimised, since after all it was nothing more than greed, it would become dominant and be sanctified as the creator of a new order, and in achieving such status it would proceed to desancitify all that had formerly held it in check.

This problem is but one of a number of other new factors to have emerged which have had adverse effects on the practical working of the democratic ethic, even to the stage of being catastrophic. The theory of democracy appears to have first emerged in ancient Greece and was based on the concept of the citizen having a free voice in determining the nature and the direction of the political process. Early Greek civilisation was a complex of small city states in which the status of citizenship was limited to a small number with the power to vote, even though that status itself rested on the economic increment produced by a large body of slaves. The number of citizens was modest enough to enable them to congregate in a common assembly and to speak and vote on the issues of the day.

In the western world such democratic practice was buried for centuries under feudalism, under arbitrary forms of royal prerogative and under the general ascendancy of a property-owning class which in turn, coupled with enormous developments of trade and industry, proceed to begin that enlargement of the powers of central government to the giant proportions that now dominate citizen life today. It prompted Rousseau, in the middle of the 18th century, to declare: 'The more the state is enlarged, the more freedom is diminished.' Rousseau was juggling with numbers in terms of thousands. Today mass societies presume to operate in democratic terms when their numbers run to millions, and even billions, and still there is an owlish disposition to assume that these swollen numbers have no effect on the basic democratic premise that the voice of the individual citizen is sovereign.

The belief in the democratic validity of government on a mass basis is so entrenched in the conditioned political reflexes of most people that it requires an enormous effort of mental readjustment to shift it. This is only too understandable; people have, in the modern era at least, always lived in societies where political discussion is conducted in terms of passionate rivalries between giant political parties, themselves exponents of all the democratic shortcomings inherent in any mass structure, where too, public comment constantly focuses on the fortunes or the defects of rival leaders, where elections are conducted in a spirit akin to a national football cup-final, and as though the personal fortunes of each individual citizen rest on the outcome, where foreign affairs are constantly discussed in terms of an enormous but quite imaginary divide between 'us', the democratic countries, and 'them' the non-, or even anti-, democratic ones. Indeed people would feel disenfranchised if they did not accept it all as real, and even proceed, although to a diminishing extent, to ally themselves to one party or another.

The fact remains there is not a shred of reality in any of the lead ideas being promoted. There are crisis moments in the life of any giant state when the personal qualities of a leader may have a decisive bearing on the outcome. In 1939 it was touch and go whether Britain would commit itself to complete opposition to Hitler's bid for world power, or whether attempts to negotiate, appease and come to some sort of accommodation with him might prevail. After Hitler's armies had overrun Belgium, Holland and much of France the appeasement camp was even stronger and the issue was even more finely balanced; it was Churchill's emergence as a national war leader with a belligerent determination to oppose Hitler which ensured the war camp prevailed.

Such moments are exceptional, and it should be noted even in this case that the ordinary citizen had no voice at all in determining Churchill's leadership; it was a decision made behind closed doors and even now the average voter has very little awareness of just how precarious the situation was.

Here and there a particular leader will put a personal stamp on a particular policy, but the general momentum of events is determined by a complex of factors including investment, interest rates, the availability of resources, transport facilities, the public moods, advertising, the media, trade figures, stock markets, foreign relations and so on. How many of these can any leader expect to control or even to change?

Money Politics

The convergence of these and others factors creates the mainstream of currents any leader must follow; any attempt to steer a contrary course will sooner or later, because of the nature of the pressures operating on his position, (none of which can be remotely described as democratic), lead to loss of office and the emergence of new leaders who are more conformist.

The policies which leaders in a *mass* democracy must follow may be mad, evil, calamitous or dangerous, but nevertheless they are prisoners of the complex of forces on which their power to influence these matters ultimately rests. Nothing exemplifies this more clearly than the phenomenal success of the scheme to promote a united federal government of Europe. The reasons for promoting it ('peace', 'progress'), fly flat in the face of the economic and military realities. Its success, if achieved, can only lead to bigger wars and greater economic instability. But the advantage it does have is of giving a more level playing field to giant investment conglomerates, now operating on global scale, to enhance their power and their profits.

No elected political leader can prevail against this, despite the enormous and inevitable unpopularity of what is involved in loss of national identity, of national ties, national traditions and the general sense of being related, immediately and historically, to a comprehensible national entity.

Indeed it is noteworthy that UK mass politics are in the grip of three major parties. The smaller one, comprised of 'Liberal Democrats', is wholly committed to supporting the EUroplot, which is doubtless one reason why it is smaller. The Conservative party has been torn asunder by a majority in its own ranks who oppose the EUroplot, and the Labour Party, currently forming the government, is clearly going the same way. What is truly remarkable is how none of their leaders *dare* oppose the Brussels exercise and its manifest contempt for the democratic ethic; the determinative factor is not the ballot box.

Rather the combination of power and money can fund political leaders' election campaigns; it can ensure patronage is deployed into appropriate channels; it can mount massive propaganda campaigns in favour of its own concerns; it can establish organisations with professional staffs to promote any change it desires to be made; and it can fund the publication of books, journals, newspapers, leaflets and other means of swamping public consciousness with its venial objectives.

So the values by which people have been indoctrinated to accept, despite the extent to which they conflict with the basic principles of Judaeo Christian culture, to say nothing of Jewish and Islamic prescript, are those of self-enrichment as adumbrated by Adam Smith. 'The City of God' is today subordinate to 'The Wealth of Nations'.

Money itself is not of course subject to any degree of democratic control at all. Given the scale on which it operates how can it be? Decisions on the amount of money in circulation, the rate at which banks charge interest, to say nothing of the shape and size of coins and notes, are all taken secretly and no attempt is made to consult those who use them.

It is money power which has established the current norms of international trade, itself a dominant force determining the pattern of millions of peoples lives, in despite of any ballot box decisions made on a mass scale. It is a pattern which, in a constant quest for immediate gain, has largely destroyed the localised means of economic self-sufficiency, a factor basic to the stability and sustainability of any democratic civilisation. Village shops in the Northern hemisphere, (where they still exist), commonly now stock basic foodstuffs from countries in the Southern hemisphere, whilst local agriculture is neglected and abandoned farms abound. Village employment is not focused on basic food production or on agriculture and farming, instead labour is absorbed in the sale and service of cars, of computers, mobile telephones and other items of factory production, all this and a great deal more dependent on a flow of relatively cheap oil.

The same basic dislocation of life is observable in the way man has been robbed of the meaning of work and divorced from the possibilities of a creative role in the use of machines. Thanks to the power of money it is now machines which use men; men wait upon the imperative demands of machine processes and unwittingly submit to a quite new form of slavery. It is the slavery of acquiescence to processes generated by the power of money man cannot control, which involves the abolition of creative endeavour, something the most primitive savage of antiquity could freely experience, as man dances upon the imperatives of machines and their allied office-routine concomitants.

It was Freud who argued that 'work is man's chief contact with reality', and the reality today is of a man or woman rising at an early hour to consume a breakfast of unnatural foodstuffs driving, with all the stresses that owning, maintaining and using a car involves, for an hour or more to a workplace, or to travel in a packed commuter train, to a workplace where attendance on machines proceeds to absorb the main mental and physical energies of his day. He returns by the same means and with the same degree of stress and tedium, to his home, where he harms his body by consuming more dead or unnatural foodstuffs, before collapsing before a TV screen busy assuring him he is living in the best of all possible worlds and one which will be ever better if only he will purchase this or that new machine, poisonous toiletry, insurance policy, foreign holiday or, wait for it, if only he will vote for this or that politician who, incidentally, is involved in the same life defeating routines which exercise not a glimmer of his creative powers.

Society Under Attack

A democratic deficit carries with it also a moral deficit, if only because democracy itself is a moral concept. In this light we need to acknowledge that a democratic deficit has a character which is quite singular in its effects and its potency. A moral deficit can take many forms and most of them will have particular effects within a particular sphere whilst enabling more positive and benign forces to continue flourish. A propensity for theft, drunkenness, slander, drug dealing, violence or swindling will ordinarily be the work of a minority in any healthy social organism, and that minority will tend to engender its own counter forces which will often be able to constrain it and enable society to continue to flourish.

A democratic deficit is different in that far from assailing the ordinary workings of a particular aspect of society it is attacking the basis of society itself, for democracy is not only the guardian angel of freedom, it is the wellspring from which all other aspects of social decency are enabled to flourish.

We have noted how one of the fundamental precepts of mainstream religious teaching centres on the injunction to 'love thy neighbour', it would indeed appear to be the primary law of any social order. It pre-supposes that you have a neighbour and that any workable social relationships are based not on hate, violence or enmity but on the readiness to practice those bonds of mutuality that engender respect, trust, concern, service and even sacrifice, and which are understood to be enshrined in the concept of love.

But in order to express love one must be free to love, and it is because the practical working of democracy is the social mechanism which is the basis of that freedom, it is also the reason why democracy is a supreme social virtue and why any deficit has results which are able to engender supreme forms of evil, forms which are beyond control until the democratic deficit is repaired.

What then is the role of those who profess to be the moral leaders of our societies, those who speak for churches, mosques, temples, synagogues, Quaker meeting houses and so on, in relation to this critical deficit? Most of them, especially the older bodies, today find themselves on the horns of a dilemma largely of their own making. Nearly all of them appear to have been founded by small groups of authoritarian zealots who sought acknowledgement of their authority, often by the use of force, as being the divinely inspired guardians of absolute truths. Those who rejected their teaching were outcasts, sinners, infidels and generally damned, and there is a profound masochistic streak in human nature which makes many only to ready to submit to the authoritarianism involved; so religious structures have generally been hierarchal, authoritarian, secretive, powerful and ever ready to resort to draconian measures to ensure conformity with their teaching. But down the centuries that teaching has changed and so too has the note of authoritarianism, and by one of histories' super-elegant ironies the agent of change has been core religious teaching itself.

It is not for nothing that it is church bodies today which are prominent in promoting human rights, gender equality, fair trade, 'peace', social justice and other apparently positive concerns stemming from and dependent upon the democratic ethic. It is Christians who have established hospitals for the sick, care homes for the orphaned, the homeless and the aged, who have helped to end the barbarities of flogging of service personnel and young people and of abolishing capital punishment.

All this work and very much more has been inspired by the teachings of Jesus of Nazareth, whose advocates, not content with the sublime miracle of that teaching, have insisted on the decorative embellishments of 'miracle' cures, walking on the water and a water into wine transformation, in order to impress the gullible and the credulous.

But that teaching had its own dynamic resonance in the democratic ethic, which is now heavily encroaching even on the institutionalised authoritarianism of church structures. So in addition to non-conformist dispositions towards congregational governance and similar moves towards democratic governing structures, Anglicans, for example, now have their 'synods' comprised not only of clergy but of elected lay people who freely debate and decide issues of church structure belief, ritual, authority and so on.

Anglicans may still find themselves in a time warp, but the worst hit of the Christians by this democratic development has been the Roman Catholic Church, now fighting a desperate rearguard battle to retain the power of Papal authority against the encroaching tide of the democratic ethic inspired by the teaching of its own founder.

What must concern us, since religious bodies continue to represent a considerable potential force, is how they relate their awakening consciousness of the imperative demands of the democratic ethic to the overwhelming shadows of the global crisis. The fact is they do not relate at all. They have virtually abdicated their role and the global crisis simply passes them by.

Today all powerful religious bodies owe their power in part to the extent to which they are part of and identified with the power of the state, a power which has largely passed to those who control the media, and if the church wants exposure in the media as guardians and leaders of moral issues and to avoid ridicule and distortion, it must conform to the values of the media. If it doesn't it is just not heard. And when it is heard it is assumed to be speaking in accord with those values. When the Church is closely identified with authority in the popular mind, especially with the authority of the state, it cannot fail to share in a general loss of prestige when the state ceases to be an effective guardian of the general public interest.

It is a situation which highlights the whole question of the moral basis of the social order; is it based on any moral imperative at all? Or is it merely an agglomeration of the impulses of self-enrichment which expresses the crude instincts of man's egoism and reduces the social order to a competitive struggle for the supremacy of what is base and ignoble?

Church teaching, and indeed any expression of religious belief, is an attempt to hold human striving to certain principles of service, and even of sacrifice, which can raise the human adventure to heights of nobility and accomplishment which have given it whatever aspects of glory and whatever distinctive refinements and loveliness of the spirit it has so far achieved. In the modern era this teaching has been swamped by rampant market forces to which, all too often, it has felt obliged passively to acknowledge rather than challenge. And of course, in consequence, it is dying, and only a robust assertion of that teaching can hope to restore it.

Promoting Democratic Money

If there is to be a change of course, if moral precept is to be raised as the governing matrix of money matters, it is evident that it cannot be done on a large, centralised scale, if only because that terrain is already occupied by our current money masters and any attempt to match their scale would simply create the basis for the same problems. No less evident is it that since morals are based above all on personal relationships, it is to the local scene where such relationships predominate that we must look.

In point of fact there is a considerable chink in the armour of giantism here, and the giants themselves have shown how it may be exploited to serve moral rather than mercenary ends. It is the giants who have demonstrated how it is possible to conduct banking operations whilst having no reserves of precious metals in their vaults at all. They simply act as depositories of peoples' notional money and, on the nominal basis of such deposits, make loans to others. These loans then of course become registered in its records as further deposits and off we go as far as the ability of borrowers to repay their loans can reach.

There is no practical reason at all why any group of people in a given locality having sufficient local repute and standing, and seriously concerned enough to do it, could not establish a local banking process, locally owned and controlled on the same working basis. If the objective were to be to establish local control they would need to insist on the principle of local residence as being the prerequisite of membership of the appropriate trust management body, they would need to insist on the same residence condition for depositors and borrowers, and in this way ensure that local control was maintained and that any surplus accruing from its operations would enrich the local economy instead of being siphoned off to some remote board-room.

The local trust could use deposits to invest in local resources and local enterprises, it could establish its own community pension fund, become a broker of local mortgages and so on. If it decided to sell shares in any Trust enterprises it would have to insist, to maintain the integrity of local ownership and control, that purchase be confined to local residents and that transfer of ownership to non-residents prohibited.

There is nothing novel about these proposals. Under a variety of names, credit unions, community trust, community currency, local money, mutual credit, Local Employment and Trading system (LETS), for example, efforts have been made to stimulate local employment and development by means of local control of local money and credit. An admirable account of some of their operations, coupled with a comprehensive survey of the theoretical background and some of their associated problems is given in Thomas H Greco's volume on 'Money'[2]

When the current oil glut shrinks to being an oil famine the local ownership and control of local resources will then develop its own increasing dynamic; local employment, local shopping and entertainment can be expected to recover much of their former vitality and the local economy could begin to reap those benefits of which it has for so long been so sedulously and silently deprived.

The issue of local ownership and control of local resources by means of local control of credit, a control which would give considerable power to a local community to determine the shape and direction of local economic development, also raises the question of a local currency. Experience has shown that such a currency can be a powerful stimulus to local economic activity, especially when a

---

[2]   *MONEY – Understanding and Creating Alternatives to Legal Tender*. Thomas H Greco, Jr. 2001. Chelsea Green Publishing Co. PO Box 428, White River Junction, UT 05001. USA ISBN 1-890132-37-3

national currency has been instrumental in creating a blight of mass unemployment and a general state of economic depression.

Whether this would be more effective as a means of controlling the general direction of economic development or not, or whether both could or should operate in tandem, as well as considering whether a local currency could beneficially run in parallel with a national currency, are questions on which there are currently no clear answers. It is a defect which helps to indicate the wide range of matters in other aspects of human scale concerns on which research and debate are badly needed. Before long perhaps some perceptive patron will come to the rescue and help to fund the establishment of an appropriate research institution as a matter of greater current urgency than any of the concerns that now appear to absorb so much of the attention of the academic world.

What perhaps deserves emphasis is why such local money controls are needed at all, and why for that matter such a research body related to them can help; on that we can say with confidence that any such steps can constitute a major advance in helping to overcome some of the principle elements of the democratic deficit, a deficit which has become such a catastrophic spanner in many of the works of modern economic statecraft.

Chapter Nine

Survival

Kinship factor. – Tribal structure. – Moral Factor of tribalism. – Religion a factor of survival. – Destructive impact of mass society in creating the global crisis. – Children at risk. – Need for Reformation. – Relate statistics of production to figures on family breakdown. – The prospects of hope and renewal.

The Religious Dimension

The most important consideration relating to the need for the empowerment of small communities has been left for a final chapter.

Every form of life on this planet, and doubtless beyond, is suffused with one overriding, imperative and inescapable necessity, the need to survive. It sits no less imperatively of course on human shoulders, and the response to that biological need has comprised the texture of human history since man first appeared on the stage.

The individual need to survive was equipped with good eyesight, good hearing, an upright posture, limbs facilitating quick movement, either for escape, defence or attack, and, apparently new in the record, swift and enlarged powers of comprehension accommodated in an unusually large brainbox.

But with all these and other attributes, a sense of smell, of touch and taste for example, they were not enough. At the hunter-gatherer level of development man developed a spirit of gregariousness. This was not just a matter of instinctive mating, for his mating was not an indiscriminate and transient pairing; in early times he must have developed a strong sense of kinship, with his partner, and also with his parents, his siblings and his progeny. The human family grouping no doubt had its origins in that overlarge brainbox with its heightened imaginative resources and its capacity for sensitivity, a sensitivity expressed uniquely in the animal kingdom for pity, compassion, loyalty and a heightened capacity for love.

One thing is apt to lead to another; if from early times the stable family unit was a biological reality because it was already a biological necessity, what then were its relations with other human family units? Were they to be rivals? Enemies? Or fellow members of an even larger grouping?

Again the necessity for survival impelled the answer. If family groups engaged in internecine fractiousness, as no doubt they often did, it exposed them to dangers from other life forms and to the realities of hunger and even starvation.

Survival needs indicated the benefits of cooperation, of joining together to obtain food, for protection and for purposes of attack. The social unit of the clan and the tribe might have been slow to evolve but it paved the way for tribes to create bonds which cohered into tribal kingdoms such as prevailed in most of Africa until the advent of the colonial era.

It is important to note that the bonds which held any particular tribe together were emphatically personal ones. Members knew each other in the round as comprehensible personalities and these bonds were the stuff which met the survival necessities of the time.

With the passage of time other factors came into play to affect those personal bonds, helped as so often by that powerful brainbox; communication developed, language evolved and with it song and dance, dress and bodily adornment, different customs of mating, cooking, customary usage, culture and with it all, a moral sense. Any human grouping needs a moral basis on which to conduct its relationships, a basis which dispels suspicion, creates trust, confidence, the assurance of fair play, justice in disputes, the capacity to relax and to socialise at ease. Such a basis is an indispensable factor in ensuring the group's cohesion and the integrity of its identity. Without the development of this moral sense man could not have developed from being a feckless brute on a mob basis.

But that super-active brainbox impelled him to speculate on the mystery of his own being; why was he here at all? If there was meaning and purpose in life then what were they? He began to envisage some transcendent meaning which soared above the bounds of his individual existence. And still that hyperactive brainbox, bewildered by the mystery of life, by the power of the sun, of rain and wind, by the tantalising glitter of the stars and the awesome progression of the seasons, impelled the need for answers. Men began to worship the incomprehensible forces that hovered beyond understanding but which must have somehow gestated the entire life story into existence. Religion was born.

All these developments sprang from and were linked to the need to survive, and it is perhaps only when viewed in such terms that the full nature of the catastrophe of our modern lifestyle becomes apparent, for in almost every respect it has been allowed to negate or destroy all the factors which once held communities together and made their survival possible.

The personal bonds which once made social units tightly knit entities and able to express a collective power and a collective will and identity have been sacrificed on the altar of a wholly new feature of human life, the *mass* society. The inherently destructive and debasing nature of mass entities and mass government are everywhere around us. It has largely destroyed the social and the survival significance of personal bonds and in doing so has greatly reduced the vital capacity of inter-personal communication, substituting for it *mass* communication.

The *mass* society is a product not of the partnership and the involvement of the general body of its members, as were all previous social structures, it is the product of a tiny minority in key positions of control addicted to the exercise of power or the quest for wealth. The mass society, of its nature, can only operate on the basis of strong centralised controls; this minority has succeeded in grasping the levers of these controls and imposing *their* needs and *their* values on the mass. The result is a global crisis of such proportions that it is now threatening the survival of the human race, nothing less.

A restoration of community life and power is thus not some idealised daydream of what might be; it is a stark imperative necessity for human survival. Societies based on personal bonds made decisions by establishing a careful choice between right and wrong, between good and evil. What was right and good was what might contribute to greater social cohesion, a greater sense of loyalty to the group and an awareness of the need to adhere to precise forms and to reject anything that might undermine the collective ethical sense. But why? Because the survival of the group depended on it. It is the key to grasping why all major religious teaching embodies the command 'love thy neighbour'.

The market forces which in three centuries or more have imposed themselves on what is called 'western civilisation', (when Gandhi was asked what he thought of it he riposted he thought it would be a very good idea), are not remotely concerned with moral choices.

In 2002 a 'Commission on Children at Risk' was established in the USA and entitled its report *Hardwired to Connect*. The Commission comprised a panel of leading children's doctors, research scientists and youth service professionals and its report urged the need for new strategies '... to reduce the currently high numbers of US children who are suffering from emotional and behavioural problems such as depression, anxiety, attention-deficit, conduct disorders and thoughts of suicide.'

Their conclusions urge that much of this increase is due to the increasing breakdown of family life from divorce, separation, single-parent child-rearing coupled with the decline of 'social connectedness' and the deterioration of significant social factors such as civic and community groups, centres of worship, political clubs and workplace associations.

All this of course is only half the story; the other half needs to be seen in the disappearance of local neighbourhood shops and trades, the ubiquity of the ultra-powerful medium of T.V., and its impact on morals, the individual sense of meaning, identity and integrity, to this must be added the virtual abolition of local government and its replacement with centrally controlled local administration.

A radical reformation of government is needed and the word 'reformation' is not misplaced. In the 16th century the Catholic Church was at the height of its power and wealth. For several centuries it had inspired an outburst of creative enterprise of such stupendous splendour that Europe became studded with schools, colleges, libraries, hospitals, churches, abbeys and above all, cathedrals, of a quality which continues to enthral the senses to this day. It was an outburst of creative wonder based on a creative awareness of the potentialities of architectural, musical and artistic beauty and backed by a degree of technical skill and learning for which centuries later we still have no parallel.

But the Church had also reached an apex of super-power corruption, for despite the wonder of its accomplishments its practice in many spheres was betraying its own teachings. A new spirit was stirring in men and ecclesiastical constraints, often heavy-handed and venial, to say nothing of a common resort to torture and extortion, made change inevitable. Either it would reform itself or reform had to come from without, and since it was incapable of achieving the former the latter became the trigger.

We are today at a similar historic stage of reformation. The modes of government which have matured over recent centuries are simply ceasing to function properly and show many signs of being incapable of functioning at all. As in the 16th century, when the challenge was not to change church policy but to change the Church itself, so today real radicals are concerned not so much to change government policy but to change the structure of government itself.

Despite the marvels of modern technology, (in some cases because of them), and the assumed advances in citizen welfare that have been achieved, government can achieve neither peace, stability nor general well-being. Figures about production and consumption will appear to reflect a growth in both and to indicate a rising tide of prosperity; such figures are achieved as though greater consumption is some overriding goal of human existence, and that when realised will answer its main problems.

But despite all the bangles and the glitter it needs to be asked, have they managed to improve the quality of life? Are people in overdeveloped countries today more relaxed, more at peace with themselves, more fulfilled and more vitally alive, more creative, enjoying happier relationships, more aware of the beauty and the miracle of natural life or more full of the wonder of the panorama of their own life experience?

Other figures, not related to the business of getting and spending, convey a rather different picture. They indicate nothing less than breakdown; breakdown of marriages and of family life, breakdown of local community structures and relationships, breakdown of peoples health, both mental and physical, and on an ever increasing scale, a breakdown of any sense of consensual moral order. Lacking any sense of control over the passage of events or over prospects of preserving peace, or of controlling economic activity so that it responds to human need rather than simply oiling the wheels of human greed. And what of deteriorating environmental conditions, the destruction of countless human cultures so that cities the world over come to reflect the bleak, bland uniformities of market imperatives rather than the creative questing of the human soul, and where cultural consciousness in every land is swamped not with the results of the unique strivings for meaning in terms of local geography, flora, fauna and climate, but with the logos and sales slogans of global merchants?

The quality of life, despite the affluence now enjoyed by a small minority of the global population, has deteriorated sharply in the last two or three generations, largely owing to the crudity of the impact of technology on our lives. For the majority of the human race economic conditions have not improved, they have worsened considerably and there are multiple signs that on our present course they cannot avoid getting worse.

The sense of this is not confined to older people, it is the young who today are the activists in Greenpeace, in Anti-war demonstrations, who organise against GM crops, in promoting Human Rights, Fair Trade, Intermediate Technology, Anti-globalisation measures, organic farming, and a host of other reformist movements. They are as aware as anyone could be that the dangers and disasters that now crowd upon the human scene have all the potentiality to overwhelm the entire adventure of civilisation.

The attempt here has been to show here the real nature of some of the forces promoting this awesome scenario and to show how they can be countered and how the means can be created for an entirely new and hopeful phase of human development. It involves a root and branch reassessment of our prevailing power structures and how they work and a recognition that no civilisation with a working basis of an ardent pursuit of the seven deadly sins can possibly long survive.

We are not here confronting darkness at noon; rather I believe we are on the threshold of an altogether new phase of human achievement. We have applied the wondrous gift of human reasoning to the science of life and from it have developed vast new technologies and powers. Today the rampant abuse of these developments now threatens to bring to a halt all the new possibilities they have helped to reveal. But we have not come all this way only to be undone by our own deeds; the challenge facing the entire spectrum of human identity and its destiny is to establish a mastery and control over these new forces.

All modern history is a tragic record of our failure to recognise that 19th century concepts of politics and statecraft, and the acceptance of giant national entities such as now hold sway in different parts of Europe, in China, Russia, India, the USA and elsewhere, are not answers to our problem, they *are* the problem. Their continuance can only accelerate and enlarge the problems their very existence has created. Far from being harbingers of progress they are barriers to it and the alternative route, that can salvage democracy and rescue civilisation, has been sketched as clearly as the author's talents permit in these pages.

But who, surveying the might and power of the forces promoting the current global scenario, can fail to ask whether a reformation as here proposed can possibly be achieved? Let them take heart; if slavery has been abolished, if torture is outlawed, if trade unions are a force, if women have gained the vote and now have equal status with men, however incompletely, if gender is now viewed in terms of an unassuming toleration of differences rather than the bigoted tendency to denigrate and defame, if racial prejudice is seen for what it is, if colonialism in many forms is now largely history, if the United Nations now has a 'Charter of Human Rights', consider that this and very much more, has been the work of dedicated and often seemingly insignificant minorities.

They have prevailed because they have sought to echo the deepest, the most pervasive and persistent longing in the human soul; the longing to be free, free to live, to create and to enrich life. They are those echelons of the spirit who have always erupted in every land to burst upon the scene to challenge settled acceptances of evil; who insist on disrupting established tyranny and degeneracy and who embrace life itself as a cause to be championed to the end, with all the impetuosity of a springtime bud bursting into flower. Despite all the odds they will prevail, if only because they are the quintessence of the spirit of life itself.

Appendix 1

There have been a number of adverse references to the role of the Church in the foregoing, and in fairness the reader may need to be reminded of the open letter sent by The Archbishop of Canterbury to the leaders of the main political parties during the 2005 general election. He wrote:

Dear Party Leader,

Despite the best of intentions, election campaigns can quickly turn into a competition about who can most effectively frighten voters with the prospect of what 'The Others' are going to do. Regrettably, there seems little reason to suppose that the general election will be immune from such temptation. Indeed, it already looks as though familiar anxieties over terrorism, asylum and immigration, and crime, are going to feature prominently in the contest.

I don't envy the task you and your colleagues face in trying to formulate responses to the real challenges here. But I hope you will seek to do so in ways that do not simply allow our fears to go unexamined.

— First: What practical initiatives can be taken to halt and reverse our collective lack of international responsibility about the environment?

— Second: What are we really prepared to do about the long-term effects of irresponsible international economic policies? There are many issues involved here of which debt is probably the most familiar, but another blindingly obvious factor, as the Africa Commission has highlighted, is the arms trade. The sale of small arms in particular makes it easier to deploy child soldiers. How is this disgrace to be brought to an end? And what sustained investment can we promise to rehabilitate children already brutalised by these conflicts?

— Third: We worry about crime, yet we often seem not to notice that the present penal system is characterised by staggeringly high levels of re-offending. Do we want punishment to change anything? Are we investing enough in the possibilities of 'restorative justice' and in first class education and rehabilitation facilities throughout the prison service? No one seems really convinced that we have a working system; building more prisons is no answer. Why not say so and propose a better way? Who's going to make history by offering a constructive alternative in penal policy, a plan that actually sets out to address offending behaviour?

— Fourth: The crime problem has a lot to do with a growing number of young people who are severely emotionally undernourished and culturally alienated. Ask anyone who works with children or young people in any city. The climate of chronic family instability, sexual chaos and exploitation, drug abuse and educational disadvantage is a lethal cocktail. To call for more public support for stable families and marriage is not in this context a bit of middle-class, Middle England nostalgia; it's life and death. To ask for public investment in skilled, properly resourced youth work is not begging for subsidised leisure; it's asking for basic human necessities. So what is the programme for fuller and better family support, fuller and better care for our children throughout society?

Is all this just religious idealism, altruistic aspiration that can't be taken too seriously? Of course I'm concerned about these things chiefly because I'm a Christian who believes that the world is to be cherished, the innocent protected and human dignity preserved. But the Bible's vision of a properly functioning society is in fact deeply realistic. Sooner or later, injustice anywhere corrupts and kills a whole community. Ignore the needs or the dignity of another and you strike at your own life and dignity in the long run.

That's something worth being afraid of.

✠ **Rowan Cantuar,** *Lambeth Palace*

Appendix 2

Annotated Bibliography

The brief essay we have entitled 'Village Democracy' has of necessity covered a very wide field; it is one which makes it impracticable to seek to detail a bibliography which covers the entire spectrum of concerns to which reference has been made. All the author can do is to indicate a few of the major contemporary sources which have been the background to his thinking and to which the reader may find some assistance in seeking his own path through the welter of literature on these concerns that now pours from the presses.

Chief and foremost of these is indubitably *The Breakdown of Nations*, by Leopold Kohr. A fundamental and scholarly text of human-scale thinking. Indispensable to all seeking the politics of the future. (Green Books in association with New European Publications, £9.95)

The Way. Edward Goldsmith's Magnum Opus, one on which he worked for 40 years to project a world view which pleads for an ecological understanding of the crisis of modern society. (Therms Books, 1992, £28.50)

A Pair of Cranks, edited by John Papworth. A succinct collection of essays by Leopold Kohr and Fritz Schumacher. (New European Publications, £10.95)

The Breakdown of Europe, Richard Body. From any standpoint a brilliant analysis of one of the most crucial issues of our time. (New European Publications, £9.95)

The Human Scale, Kirkpatrick Sale. A monumental survey of how the social disease of giantomania has created the ever burgeoning crisis of US life, and a detailed call for action by the foremost radical author of the English speaking world. (Perigee Books, £15.95)

In The Absence of the Sacred, Jerry Mander. A skewering critique of modern technology, in which cars, telephones, computers, banks, biogenetics and television ... all are shown to be part of a mad 'megatechnology' that is destroying the world's resources and robotizing its people. (Sierra Club Books, £19.95)

Retrieved From The Future, John Seymour. The great John Seymour's last great book, a novel depicting the civil war which erupted when organised civil life was shattered by the global economic collapse. (New European Publications, £9.95)

Five Holocausts, Derek J Wilson. A masterly detailed depiction of the major crisis factors of our time. (Steele Roberts Ltd., New Zealand, £15.95.)

Crisis Wisdom, edited by John Papworth. An indispensable collection of 'quotes' from the sages of the human scale. (The Fourth World, 2001, £12.95)

All available from:

> The Fourth World
> Box 2410
> Swindon
> Wiltshire
> SN5 4XN
> UK

(Cheques THE FOURTH WORLD). They help to create a new groundwork of the kind of thinking we need to embrace if the current crisis is to be resolved.

A number of journals also seek to promote much the same views from other perspectives, notably:

Adbusters. An invaluable Canadian-based attempt to explore the realities of life behind the facade of advertising and of contemporary consumerist values. (1243 W 7th Avenue, Vancouver BC, V6H 1B7)

The Ecologist. An indispensable monthly commentary on the leading environmental issues of the day. (18 Chelsea Wharf, Lots Road, London, SW10 OQJ)

Fourth World Review. First established forty years ago, a bimonthly compendium of trenchant criticism of current suicidal social trends and diverse proposals for regeneration. (Box 2401, Swindon, Wilts, SN5 4XN)

Index

SOCIETAS: essays in political and cultural criticism

Public debate has been impoverished by two competing trends. On the one hand the trivialization of the media means that in-depth commentary has given way to the ten second soundbite. On the other hand the explosion of knowledge has increased specialization, and academic discourse is no longer comprehensible. As a result writing on politics and culture is either superficial or baffling.

This was not always so — especially for political debate. The high point of the English political pamphlet was the seventeenth century, when a number of small printer-publishers responded to the political ferment of the age with an outpouring of widely-accessible pamphlets and tracts. But in recent years the tradition of the political pamphlet has declined—with most publishers rejecting anything under 100,000 words. The result is that many a good idea ends up drowning in a sea of verbosity. However the introduction of the digital press makes it possible to re-create a more exciting age of publishing. *Societas* authors are all experts in their own field, but the essays are for a general audience. Each book can be read in an evening. The books are available retail at the price of £8.95/$17.90 each, or on bi-monthly subscription for only £5/$10. Details/updated schedule at **imprint-academic.com/societas**

IMPRINT ACADEMIC, PO Box 200, Exeter, EX5 5YX, UK
Tel: (0)1392 841600   Fax: (0)1392 841478   sandra@imprint.co.uk